A LANCASHIRE
MISCELLANY

A LANCASHIRE MISCELLANY

TOM HOLMAN

FRANCES LINCOLN LIMITED
PUBLISHERS
www.franceslincoln.com

For Sam

Frances Lincoln Limited
4 Torriano Mews
Torriano Avenue
London NW5 2RZ
www.franceslincoln.com

A Lancashire Miscellany
Copyright © Frances Lincoln Limited 2010
Text copyright © Tom Holman 2010

First Frances Lincoln edition 2010

A catalogue record for this book is available from the British Library.

ISBN 978-0-7112-3093-4

Printed and bound in Hong Kong

1 2 3 4 5 6 7 8 9

A THREE-MINUTE HISTORY OF LANCASHIRE

Celts, Britons, Romans, Anglo-Saxons, Vikings and the Normans – all these people and more have helped to shape and strengthen Lancashire over the course of its long, turbulent and fascinating history.

Plenty of evidence of Stone Age life has been found across the county, and the fertile Ribble Valley in particular has signs of inhabitation going back at least ten thousand years. Early hunters and gatherers would have found the area densely forested and wild, but swathes of it were cut down to make way for agriculture after the Celts arrived in Iron Age Lancashire in the shape of two related tribes: the Brigantes, who tended to settle in the north, and the Carvelli, who gathered along the coast.

The Romans arrived in Britain in AD 43, but did not establish themselves in Lancashire until the 70s, when they built their first fort at Ribchester. More settlements followed at or near what are now Manchester, Lancaster, Kirkham, Warrington and Wigan, and the roads they built between these places formed the basis for the county's transport infrastructure.

The Celtic people who settled again across the county after the departure of the Romans in the early 5th century now developed distinct settlements, the names of which evolved into many modern-day Lancashire towns and cities. Next came the Anglo-Saxons, and by the 7th century Lancashire was part of both the Kingdom of Northumbria and, from south of the River Ribble, the Kingdom of Mercia. The Saxons soon converted to Christianity, and traces of their religion including distinctive crosses can be seen on a handful of church sites today.

The period of calm and security that followed was ended by the arrival of the Vikings, who imposed themselves on the area either by force or alliance with the now-subjugated local rulers. But having settled in, they also advanced agriculture and trade in the region and, like the Anglo-Saxons, added their influence to its place names and institutions. By the time of the Norman Conquest in 1066, Lancashire was roughly divided into a handful of regions, parcelled up by King William for his barons. The new ruler chose Lancaster as his headquarters, and by the middle of the 12th century the area was becoming known as the county of Lancashire. A century later, Lancashire became an earldom and then, in 1351, a dukedom. It was now a county palatine, meaning that it had royal powers and could develop its own ruling and legal structures with some independence from the King.

Once tensions between the Normans and Anglo-Saxons had eased, the county began to develop something like its modern character, with markets helping towns to grow in size and land enclosures delineating the countryside. Stability in the region was again interrupted by the Wars of the Roses from around 1455 onwards. Mostly because of its geographical position, Lancashire was somewhat isolated from the rest of England over the next few hundred years, and its sense of separation grew during the Reformation, when large parts remained defiantly Catholic despite the adoption of Protestantism elsewhere. Divisions in the county grew wider with the English Civil Wars, and Lancashire was host to several major battles between Royalists and Parliamentarians through the 1640s.

Afterwards, Lancashire developed further as a largely rural county until the Industrial Revolution brought explosive change from the late 18th century onwards. Towns sprawled to accommodate new manufacturing and mining industries, ports grew as trade flourished, and new rail links brought previously remote areas of the county much closer together. While a handful of Lancastrians made fortunes, millions more suffered in dreadful conditions at work and home. These slowly improved over the 19th century, and the increased money and leisure time fuelled the growth of seaside resorts like Blackpool.

The subsequent decline of its adopted industries, plus the loss of life and upheaval from two world wars, threatened to bring Lancashire to its knees. But new industries and the effect of post-war immigration have created yet another Lancashire - a county that juxtaposes dramatic rural beauty and vibrant urban life like few others in England. Its boundaries have been endlessly tweaked by reorganisations of local government, not least in 1974 when the modern administrative county was substantially reduced in size. But most Lancastrians aware of their history identify with the county palatine as it was at its creation - and their sense of loyalty and love of Lancashire is as powerful as it has ever been.

LANCASHIRE FOOD – HOT POT

No meal is more evocative of Lancashire than the traditional, hearty and satisfying Hot Pot.

At its simplest, Hot Pot is a cheap, easily prepared stew of lamb or mutton and onions, topped by slices of potato. Its exact origins are unknown, but it probably has its roots among the mill and factory workers of the region who might assemble it in the morning and put it on to cook slowly all day, giving them a steaming hot meal ready for their return at the end of their shift. Cooked Hot Pots – the name refers to the heavy dish in which it was cooked – would also be kept warm in blankets for a picnic later in the day, perhaps at work in factories, mines or fields, or on days out at the races.

Perhaps because of its humble origins and cheap ingredients, Lancashire Hot Pot has sometimes been looked down on as a dish, but the rising interest in local food has brought it firmly back into fashion, and it can now be found on plenty of pub and restaurant menus in Lancashire and beyond. Because it is so easy to prepare in advance, it is also a convenient supper with little washing up for anyone who – like the mill workers of the past – is too busy or tired to prepare anything from scratch at the end of a long day.

Like all cherished local dishes the precise recipe for Lancashire Hot Pot is the subject of intense debate, and there are as many variations on the basic formula as there are cooks in the county. Lambs' kidneys, slices of black pudding or oysters are sometimes added to the meat, vegetables like carrots, turnips or leeks may be used to pad out the stew, and herbs or red wine added to enhance the gravy. This version is fairly true to the traditional Hot Pot.

A recipe for Lancashire Hot Pot
(serves four to six, depending on hunger levels)
1 kg neck of lamb
1.5 kg potatoes (floury ones like Maris Piper work best)
400 g onions
600 ml stock (hot water will do)
50 g butter
2 tsp thyme leaves
Salt and freshly ground black pepper

First, assemble all your ingredients. Trim the lamb of excess fat, and cut it into rough chunks. Peel and slice the potatoes into rounds roughly quarter of an inch (0.5 cm) thick. Roughly slice the onions. Pick and chop the thyme.

Now you're ready to prepare the Hot Pot. Butter the base and sides of a deep, heavy casserole dish (an 8 pint / 4.5 litre one is ideal). Now arrange a layer of potato slices on the bottom, overlapping slightly. Scatter in half the lamb, onions and thyme, and season generously with salt and pepper. Level and top this mixture with another layer of potato slices. Scatter in the remaining lamb, onions and thyme, and season generously again. Finish with a neat layer of potato slices. Pour the stock over the Hot Pot, and dot the top with butter.

Clamp the casserole lid on tight, and bake in a low oven (160°C / 325°F / gas mark 3) for at least two hours, or longer on an even lower heat if you like. Half an hour before you're ready to eat, take the lid off the Hot Pot and turn the heat up (to 220°C / 425°F / gas mark 7) to crisp up the top layer of potatoes. Serve with the classic Lancashire Hot Pot accompaniment of pickled red cabbage.

LANCASHIRE'S FIVE CITIES

England has 50 places that, by virtue of a royal charter, can call themselves cities. Lancashire – taken here to mean the ancient and traditional county rather than the modern administrative area – has five of them. In order of the year of their official incorporation, the five cities of Lancashire are:

Lancaster (pre-dates historical records)

Manchester (1853)

Liverpool (1880)

Salford (1926)

Preston (2002)

Of these five, the largest in terms of population are Liverpool, with around 470,000 people living within its city boundaries at the 2001 Census; and Manchester, with 394,000. Populations for the wider urban areas around both cities are much higher.

THE STORY OF THE RED ROSE

Instantly recognisable to Lancastrians everywhere, the red rose is a powerful and cherished symbol of the county.

The exact origins of its association with Lancashire are the subject of some debate, but it was probably first put to symbolic use by Edmund, the first Earl of Lancaster, in the 13th century. Officially called *rosa gallica officilanis*, it may have been the first ever cultivated rose, used by the Romans and Greeks for medicinal and fragrancy purposes, and possibly first brought to England by Edmund when he returned home with his French second wife. When Edmund died, his tomb in Westminster Abbey was engraved with roses and painted red.

The symbolism of the red rose increased with his successors, but it was the Wars of the Roses in the second half of the 15th century that forever entwined it with the county. The battles were not known as such until much later, and it is unlikely that those fighting actually did so under the emblems of the roses – red for the men of Lancaster and white for those of York. Nevertheless, their symbolic importance was acknowledged by the Lancastrian Henry VII who, in a gesture of unity after emerging from the wars on top, combined the red and white roses of Lancaster and York into what is now known as the Tudor rose. It is not lost on either Lancastrians or Yorkshiremen, however, that the large red petals of the Tudor rose entirely surround the smaller white ones.

Although the House of Lancaster actually had little to do with the county of Lancashire – in fact, the Duchy's land was, and still is, spread far across England – the red rose continued to be associated with the area after the wars. Men fighting in subsequent battles adopted it as a heraldic device, most prominently and poignantly in the First World War. The Duke of Lancaster's Regiment still carries it at the heart of its cap badge.

The rose has since become shorthand for all things Lancastrian, used to enhance any concept that requires association with the county. It is incorporated into coats of arms for various councils, proudly displayed by local societies and businesses, added to the designs of shopping centres and worn by sports teams including Lancashire County Cricket Club. Any cricket match with Yorkshire – and indeed just about any sporting fixture between clubs from either side of the Pennines – is still inevitably billed as the latest installment of the ongoing war of the roses, proof of the enduring power of the symbol.

The red rose also adorns Lancashire's official flag, and is worn particularly proudly on Lancashire Day each year. The exact designs of the rose now vary somewhat, but it essentially comprises five large outer petals, separated by green leaves and with a small centre of white or yellow stamens. The original real-life variety is available to buy from garden centres and nurseries across the county.

LANCASHIRE'S SIX HUNDREDS

Centuries before it was carved up into its current jumble of administrative counties, Lancashire was, like many other parts of the country, divided into hundreds.

The beginnings of the system of hundreds are unclear, though they may have been introduced by the Saxons and, in a rough early form, pre-date the creation of Lancashire itself. Hundred status was conferred on an area either because it had more than a hundred households or because its land was sufficient to sustain that number of people. As areas grew, the hundreds were further sub-divided, though they all came to be brought under the umbrella of their shire county.

Each hundred had some control over its administration and justice systems, and their network of courts survived well into the 19th century. Although most other traces of the English hundreds have now disappeared, the names of some of them survive in local government districts. Lancashire's six hundreds and their rough boundaries were:

Amounderness – from north of Lancaster to south of Preston and out west to the Fylde coast. It included the modern-day districts of Fylde, Wyre, Preston and Ribble Valley

Blackburn – from east of Preston to the border with Yorkshire

Leyland – the 'heart' of Lancashire, from south of Preston to Standish

Lonsdale – the Furness Peninsula and into the southern Lake District; and the northern part of the county from Lancaster upwards. Probably the largest of the six, Lonsdale may once have been divided into north and south regions

Salford – roughly where Greater Manchester now stands

West Derby – most of southwest Lancashire including modern-day Merseyside

TEN CASTLES

Lancashire's history of conflict has left it with dozens of castles, towers and other fortified buildings. Here are ten of the most interesting, some largely intact and others now ruins, but all accessible or at least visible to the public.

Clitheroe Castle. Built on limestone above the town towards the end of the 12th century, the castle has a long and fascinating history, not least during the English Civil War. Parts of the castle are open to the public, as is a newly restored museum.

Dalton Castle. Small town-centre peel tower, built in the 14th century to help defend Furness Abbey. Now owned by the National Trust.

Gleaston Castle, near Barrow-in-Furness. The crumbling ruins of the towers are all that is left of this castle, built in the 14th century but already in disrepair by the 16th. Access is restricted, but the ruins can be seen from the adjacent road.

Greenhalgh Castle, near Garstang. Built by the first Earl of Derby in 1490 and largely wrecked during a Civil War siege, much of its stone taken for other nearby buildings. A single crumbling tower remains.

Hoghton Tower, near Preston. Somewhere between a manor house and a castle, this spectacular fortified hilltop building originally dates to 1109. It was badly damaged in the Civil War but restored in the 16th century. Famous guests have included several kings and queens.

Hornby Castle, near Lancaster. Much of the castle dates from a 19th-century rebuilding in the Gothic style, though the original dates back to at least the 13th century. It is now privately owned but opens on a few weekends each year.

Lancaster Castle. On a hilltop in the centre of the city, the castle has a keep, tower and gatehouse dating to the 12th, 14th and 15th centuries respectively, and boasts a long and frequently grisly history as a court and prison. While it is still used as such, large parts of the building are open to the public.

Lever Castle, Rivington. Never actually a working castle at all, this was built in the 1910s by the Lancastrian philanthropist William Lever as a replica of Liverpool Castle, which had been destroyed two centuries earlier. Work on it was never finished after Lever's death, leaving it – perhaps intentionally – as an atmospheric ruin.

Piel Castle, near Barrow-in-Furness. Fortification on Piel Island built to guard Barrow against pirates and raiders. Looked after by English Heritage and accessible via a ferry service from the mainland.

Turton Tower. The 15th-century peel tower here was extended into a fortified manor house in the Tudor period. It was another of the many Lancashire residences to see action during the Civil War.

TEN AMUSING PLACE NAMES

Lancashire has more than its fair share of unusual place names, many of them amusing to visitors if not always to the people who live there. Here are ten such places, all featured on Ordnance Survey maps.

Bare (near Morecambe)

Bedlam (near Oswaldtwistle)

Butt Hill (near Garstang)

Buttock (near Clitheroe)

Chew Moor (near Bolton)

Hey (near Colne)

Little Tongues (Fleetwood)

Nob End (near Bolton)

Ramsbottom (near Bury)

Whalley (near Clitheroe)

LANCASHIRE DAY

For all true Lancastrians, 27 November is the day to celebrate the heritage of their home county. Chosen to commemorate the date in 1295 on which the first elected representatives from Lancashire travelled south to Westminster to join King Edward I's fledgling model parliament, it is now widely known as Lancashire Day.

The event was the idea of the Friends of Real Lancashire, a group set up to protect and promote what it regards as the traditional borders of the county. Lancashire's boundaries have been the subject of much confusion following changes in England's administrative counties, most notably in 1974 when local government was overhauled. The Friends of Real Lancashire invite people to ignore these new borders, and instead regard their county as stretching as far north as Coniston in the Lake District, as far south as Manchester and as far west as Liverpool – all places that, since the borders were rejigged, are now placed outside of Lancashire on some maps. Lancashire Day is a useful occasion to promote the Friends' cause and remind people of the history and scope of the 'true' Lancashire. Though few might care to admit it, the day was also launched partly in order to catch up with the county's great rival across the Pennines, which has staged a Yorkshire Day every year since 1975.

Since it was observed for the first time in the 1990s, Lancashire Day has been celebrated in cities, towns and villages across the county, and has won support from local councils, businesses and MPs. Red roses are worn, and at 9 p.m. GMT Lancashire residents and ex-pats across the world are invited to raise a toast to 'the Queen, Duke of Lancaster'. People are also invited to recite the Lancashire Day Proclamation, as bellowed by town criers, as follows:

'To the people of the City and County Palatine of Lancaster, greetings!

Know ye that this day, November 27 in the year of our Lord two thousand and [year], in the reign of Her Majesty Queen Elizabeth II, Duke of Lancaster, is Lancashire Day.

Know ye also, and rejoice, that by virtue of Her Majesty's County Palatine of Lancaster, the citizens of the Hundreds of Lonsdale, North and South of the Sands, Amounderness, Leyland, Blackburn, Salford and West Derby are forever entitled to style themselves Lancastrians.

Throughout the County Palatine, from the Furness Fells to the River Mersey, from the Irish Sea to the Pennines, this day shall ever mark the peoples' pleasure in that excellent distinction – true Lancastrians, proud of the Red Rose and loyal to our Sovereign Duke.

God bless Lancashire and God save the Queen, Duke of Lancaster!'

LANCASHIRE'S HIGHEST POINTS

Depending on how they look at it, walkers can claim any one of three fell tops as the highest point in Lancashire. In the modern-day administrative county, the honour usually falls to Green Hill, which reaches 2,060 feet (628 m). A few miles east of Kirkby Lonsdale, it is situated on a slim finger of Lancashire right on the border with Yorkshire. Close by – but a few hundred yards inside the red rose county and so rivaling it for the highest point – is Gragareth, marked on some maps as Leck Fell, and a fraction lower at 2,057 feet (627 m). The summit is marked by an Ordnance Survey trig point, and not far away are a trio of cairns known as the Three Men of Gragareth.

Not far east of both tops is Whernside, which at 2,415 feet (736 m) is Yorkshire's second highest point and one of its Three Peaks. Yorkshire has dozens more peaks higher than Green Hill and Gragareth, and by the standards of its neighbours Lancashire is not a mountainous county. But measured by its historic boundaries, Lancashire's highest point is nearly 600 feet (183 m) higher than Green Hill and nearly 230 feet (70 m) higher than Whernside. At 2,634 feet (803 m), The Old Man of Coniston is now more usually bracketed with the Lake District or Cumbria, but until the reorganisation of county boundaries it was officially part of Lancashire's territory. Despite the changes to the boundaries, and along with other fells in the Furness range, true Lancastrians still firmly consider it to be one of their own.

LANCASHIRE'S PEOPLE IN NUMBERS

Measured by its modern-day county council borders only – and therefore excluding large swathes of 'true' Lancashire, including large cities like Manchester and Liverpool – the red rose county is home to about 1.1 million people. The 2001 Census and subsequent surveys break down Lancashire's population as follows:

1,134,976 . . . . number of people

51.5 . . . . percentage of population who are female

25.6 . . . . percentage aged 0 to 19

7.1 . . . . percentage aged 75 and over

1,048 . . . . . . people living per square mile (2.6 sq km) in Lancashire

10,540 . . . . . people living per square mile (2.6 sq km) in Blackpool, the most densely populated area of the county

260 . . . . people living per square mile (2.6 sq km) in the Ribble Valley, the least densely populated area of the county

17.9 . . . . percentage increase in population since 1961

1,364,100 . . . . projected population in 2031

8 . . . . percentage of population not born in England

7.3 . . . . percentage from black, Asian, Chinese, mixed or other ethnic groups

78.3 . . . . percentage describing their religion as Christian

52.7 . . . . percentage of adults who are married or re-married

20 . . . . percentage of adults who are separated, divorced or widowed

27.3 . . . . percentage of adults who are single

21,705 . . . . people living in medical, care
or other supported establishments
1,050 . . . . members of the armed forces stationed in Lancashire
75.2 . . . . percentage of working age population in employment
30.1 . . . . percentage leaving education with no qualifications
20.2 . . . . percentage with limiting long-term illness
23,480 . . . . median gross annual pay in pounds
among all full-time employees
491,466 . . . . household spaces
2.4 . . . . average number of people per household
12 . . . . percentage of households without central heating
29.6 . . . . . . percentage of households with two or more cars or vans
25.1 . . . . percentage of households with no car or van

GREAT LANCASTRIANS – THE BEATLES

Liverpool isn't part of the modern administrative territory of
Lancashire, but it is, with Manchester, one of the two major cities of the
traditional county. And it produced what is undoubtedly Lancashire's
most successful and widely known cultural export – The Beatles.

Although founding members Pete Best and Stuart Sutcliffe were born
elsewhere, the four main Beatles – John Lennon, Paul McCartney,
George Harrison and Ringo Starr – were all born in Liverpool between
1940 and 1943. The band grew out of The Quarrymen, the group in
which Lennon and McCartney both played after they met in the
incongruous setting of a parish fete in the Liverpool suburb of Woolton
in 1957. The Beatles' sound developed in venues across the city, most
notably at the Cavern and Casbah Coffee clubs; and in Hamburg,
Germany, where they played several residencies in the early 1960s.

Although their first releases met with only minor success, from 1963
until their last proper concert in 1966, Beatlemania swept out of
Liverpool and across the UK. Their heyday as a performing band was
short but furiously intense, the gruelling touring schedule interrupted
only by frequent studio albums and spin-off films, and they dominated
the music charts like no band before or since. Starting with 'From Me
To You' in 1963 and ending with 'The Ballad of John and Yoko' six years
later, The Beatles had 17 UK number one singles, as well as 15 number
one albums. In the US, where the group first toured in 1964, they had
20 number one singles, and at one point that year occupied the top five
positions on the chart and 12 of the top 100.

From 1967 until their split in 1970, The Beatles withdrew from the pressures of touring and performing live to concentrate on their recorded music, their sound evolving all the time despite tensions within the band and a series of controversies. By this time the group had of course grown well beyond their Lancashire roots, but they had returned to Liverpool to play often, and namechecked two city locations in their 1967 double A-side single 'Penny Lane' and 'Strawberry Fields Forever'. Any hopes of a reunion of the band ended with the murder of Lennon in New York in 1980, but there have been endless Beatles re-releases, compilations, merchandise, video games and other spin-offs ever since, as well as various solo projects. Sales of the band's music remain enormous today.

Liverpool is packed with places paying tribute to The Beatles, and it is hard to escape their influence on the city. The main place of pilgrimage for fans is The Beatles Story (tel 0151 709 1963 or visit www.beatlesstory.com), and the city also has a bus tour of locations significant to the band, inevitably billed as the Magical Mystery Tour. The childhood homes of Lennon and McCartney, owned by the National Trust, are both open to the public, as are the Casbah and Cavern clubs. For an overnight visit, Beatles addicts can try the four-star Hard Day's Night Hotel near the Cavern.

THE RISE AND FALL OF THE RAILWAY

Lancashire isn't the home of the railway, but it did do more than any other county to fuel the extraordinary growth of the British network over the 19th century.

From the start of the century onwards, small lines had been built across Britain, most notably George Stephenson's Stockton and Darlington Railway in the northeast. But it was the 1830 opening of the Liverpool and Manchester Railway – the first timetabled and steam-driven inter-city service anywhere in the world – that really got the rail movement going. It was funded by rich merchants in both cities and built to serve Lancashire's burgeoning industries, taking raw materials from the port of Liverpool in the west to the mill towns in the east. With miles of boggy valley to navigate, dozens of bridges and viaducts and a tunnel at the Liverpool end, its construction was an incredible feat of engineering for the time.

The line was an instant success, its convenience, cheap fares and novelty value making it popular among passengers as well as the merchants and mill owners. And having proved its viability here, the railway network now grew at a furious rate, with lines shooting out across the country. The 1840s was the decade of 'railway mania' – a frenzy of track-laying as investors poured money into hundreds of new train companies, backed by a sympathetic government and an excited public. Lancashire's combination of industry and a large population was particularly attractive, bringing it endless branch lines to connect even the smallest towns and villages.

Like stock market bubbles since, much of the speculation was hopelessly optimistic, and businessmen and ordinary family investors lost fortunes in companies that never got off the ground and lines that were never built. More than 6,000 miles (9,650 km) of new lines were laid in just three years in the mid-1840s, and while some of them were quickly profitable, it was clear that others would struggle to pay their way.

And almost as quickly as they rose in Lancashire, the steam railways fell. For a century after the years of railway mania, the network had consolidated, first into a handful of large operators and then under government ownership. But the decline of industry and the rise of the car sent freight journeys and passenger numbers tumbling, and many of the county's small branch lines were quietly wound down. Of those that battled on, many could not survive the government's rail rationalisation programme before and after the Beeching Report of 1963, which closed swathes of Lancashire's network. In the early 1950s, Britain had around 21,000 miles (33,800 km) of tracks and 6,000 stations; by 1975 it had 12,000 miles (19,315 km) of rails and 2,000 stations.

As diesel succeeded coal as the preferred fuel, Lancashire's once proud stock of steam engines fell too: from nearly 1,900 locomotives in 1950 to just 800 in 1965. Then, in August 1968, it hosted the last ever steam-powered passenger services on the British timetables, when two engines departed Preston for Blackpool and Liverpool. Lancashire retains a substantial network of lines, of course, and several of the abandoned tracks and locomotives have since been revived by steam enthusiasts – but its long lists of closed stations and lines are proof that the railway's glory days are now long gone.

One of the best places to find out more about the Liverpool and Manchester Railway and Lancashire's rail history in general is the Museum of Science and Industry, housed on the site of Manchester's original rail terminus at Liverpool Road (tel 0161 832 2244 or visit www.mosi.org.uk). Many of the stations along the Railway have closed, but it remains in use as a link between the cities.

LANCASHIRE'S FLAG

Flown proudly by loyal residents, Lancashire's flag bears its famous red rose set on a yellow background. Why yellow? Because by the time the Friends of Real Lancashire got round to registering a design with the Flag Institute, the agency responsible for giving flags official status, it found that a red rose on white background had already been registered – by the t own of Montrose on the east coast of Scotland. Looking for an alternative, the Friends group borrowed the tone of gold from Lancashire's official coat of arms. Since it registered the flag in 2008, the group has campaigned for it to be prominently displayed across the county.

LANCASHIRE'S FOOTBALL CLUBS

Even if its centres of power officially lie elsewhere, Lancashire has good reason to consider itself the home of English football. Measured by its traditional, ceremonial borders, the county has no fewer than 15 of the 92 teams in the four divisions of England's football league – more than any other area of the country including London. In order of their official formation, Lancashire's 15 football clubs are:

Bolton Wanderers (1874)

Blackburn Rovers (1875)

Blackpool (1877)

Everton (1878)

Manchester United (1878)

Manchester City (1880)

Preston North End (1881)

Burnley (1882)

Bury (1885)

Accrington Stanley (1891, reformed 1968)

Liverpool (1892)

Oldham Athletic (1895)

Rochdale (1907)

Morecambe (1920)

Wigan Athletic (1932)

WRITERS FROM LANCASHIRE

Lancashire has a long and rich literary tradition and has produced dozens of famous novelists, poets, playwrights and non-fiction specialists. Here are 30 of the best known, together with their places of birth.

William Ainsworth (Manchester)
Beryl Bainbridge (Liverpool)
Laurence Binyon (Lancaster)
Alan Bleasdale (Liverpool)
Ben Brierley (Failsworth)
Anthony Burgess (Manchester)
Frances Hodgson Burnett (Manchester)
Neville Cardus (Rusholme)
Richmal Crompton (Bury)
Shelagh Delaney (Salford)
J.G. Farrell (Liverpool)
Walter Greenwood (Salford)
Trevor Griffiths (Manchester)
Felicia Hemans (Liverpool)
James Hilton (Leigh)
Anna Jacobs (Rochdale)
Howard Jacobson (Manchester)
Roger McGough (Liverpool)
Jimmy McGovern (Liverpool)
Brian Patten (Liverpool)
Lynda la Plante (Liverpool)
Thomas de Quincey (Manchester)
Willy Russell (Whiston)
Dodie Smith (Whitefield)
A.J.P. Taylor (Southport)
Francis Thompson (Preston)
Salley Vickers (Liverpool)
Alfred Wainwright (Blackburn)
Edwin Waugh (Rochdale)
Jeanette Winterson (Manchester)

A LANCASHIRE DICTIONARY PART ONE:
A TO E

Drawing on influences from across the county and down the centuries, Lancashire's dialect is one of the richest and most interesting in England. It is a way of speaking that is generally inherited rather than learned – occasionally baffling to the outsider and virtually impossible to assimilate. It also varies considerably from region to region and even town to town, those in the north of the county borrowing heavily from Cumbrian words and phrases, for instance, while accents in the south are distinctively Mancunian or Liverpudlian. Scouse, indeed, has a lexicon all of its own.

What all parts of Lancashire have in common, though, is that their inflections and vocabularies have remained intact, while those in many other counties have faded away into standard English. Some popular words of the past are falling out of use, but other colloquialisms and phrases remain widely spoken – not all of them unique to Lancashire, of course, but each helping to make the language and culture here distinct and special. Here is a list of some of the more commonly heard words, together with their translations.

aam to mock
abide suffer, tolerate
aboon above
addle to earn
afore before
agate going
alreet all right
anent against
any road anyway
'appen perhaps, maybe
'appy 'arry a miserable person
art are you
awce to begin
aye yes

babby baby
back end autumn and winter of a year
badly ill (worse than simply poorly)
baggin' meal, usually the main one of the day

band string
bangle to waste time
bant to beat
bantlin' baby or toddler
barmpot a daft person
beawt without
bedfast laid up in bed
bellin' to cry out, bellow
benny tantrum
best better
bing to sour or spoil
bit a little while, soon
blather to talk nonsense or at length
bo' ball
bobby dazzler an attractive person
bog-eyed weary
boggart ghost or evil spirit
bonny beautiful
born days lifetime

bransen uncomfortably full from food
brass money
brast to burst
breet bright
brew used as a noun, a cup of tea
buckle to to set to something
bucko fighting man
bullock to cheat or bully
bump bankrupt
bunce to share
butty sandwich or buttered bread

cack-handed clumsy
cakehole mouth
chaff to tease
champion very good or great
cheer chair
childer children
chimbly chimney
chuck chicken; a term of endearment
chunner to mutter
clarty sticky, filthy
cleek to snatch
clemmed very hungry
clooas clothes

cluttermuck a very clumsy person
cob strange, different
collop slice
comer a newcomer from outside the region
cop catch
cowd cold
cow slavver cow dung
crack talk, conversation
cracky a daft person
cratchy very irritable

dateless stupid
deawldy miserable
dee to die
deet to dirty
dig duck
do a social occasion or party
dollop a quantity
drop cork-legged to be very surprised
drucken drunk
dule devil

eawl-leet owl-light; dusk
een eyes
enoo enough
ettin eaten

BESIDE THE SEASIDE

Whether remembered with fondness or dread, the Great British seaside holiday has a special place in the country's heritage – and nowhere is it more deeply ingrained than in Lancashire.

The beach holiday here grew largely out of the tradition of wakes weeks – time set aside each summer for people to enjoy the sunshine and some hard-earned leisure time. The weeks may have had some religious connotations when they started, perhaps coinciding with festivals or church anniversaries, and they proved remarkably resilient through tumultuous eras like the Industrial Revolution, during which many Lancastrians found their work changing from rural, cottage industries to vast cotton mills in the towns. Perhaps because of the long hours and unpleasant conditions they now faced, the prospect of a week's holiday became ever more precious. The wakes week was also a link with the past – a cherished tradition at a time when so many other aspects of life were changing.

A handful of places along Lancashire's Fylde coast had already become popular among the well-to-do by the end of the 18th century, with small guesthouses and hotels serving those who wanted to take the bracing sea air. But it was another consequence of the Industrial Revolution – the mushrooming of the rail network – that brought Lancashire's seaside firmly within reach of the masses. Towns like Morecambe, Lytham and St Annes grew into bustling resorts, but the capital of the Lancashire coast was undoubtedly Blackpool, where three piers, a promenade, gardens, tower, tram system and the famous street lights were all put up within 30 years in the late 19th century.

For a week at a time, Lancashire's mill towns would successively empty, often almost entirely, while their residents joyfully decamped to the guesthouses, beaches and promenades of the coast. Donkey rides, Punch and Judy shows, music halls and seaside food like fish and chips, ice cream and candyfloss all became ingredients of the British seaside holiday as workers enjoyed a week-long glimpse of a more relaxed, prosperous and happy life.

Given the notorious demands placed on workers by Lancashire's mill owners, the tradition of the wakes week must have had an extremely strong pull to survive. It endured well beyond the era of the mills, too, with factories and schools juggling their holiday schedules to accommodate the weeks. Some continued to do so even into the 21st century, and while it may no longer be widely known as such, the tradition of communities taking the same wakes week's holiday is still in evidence in some towns.

Just as rail travel brought holidaymakers to the coast, so air travel took them away again, to warmer and more exotic climes. Towns like Blackpool and Morecambe are in some ways now shadows of their former selves, with a melancholy air and reminders of their more glamorous days all around. But they remain a popular destination for many, and some resorts are reporting steadily rising visitor numbers, thanks perhaps to surging nostalgia and an awareness that home-grown holidays offer a cheaper, greener alternative to the Med. Blackpool has also tried to stir up nostalgia for wakes weeks by staging special steam train journies to the coast, and putting on special events and exhibitions for visitors when they get there.

LANCASHIRE'S PRIME MINISTERS

Lancashire has produced four of the 52 Prime Ministers of Britain since Sir Robert Walpole became the first to hold the role in a recognisable form in 1721. Two Conservatives and two Liberals, they include some significant leaders and notable reformers. Lancashire's four PMs are:

Sir Robert Peel (1788-1850), born in Ramsbottom, near Bury. Tory Prime Minister from 1834 to 1835, and again from 1841 to 1846.
The son of a rich Lancastrian mill owner, Peel is credited with substantial social reform. As Home Secretary, he launched the first recognisable force of police, still known as 'bobbies' in his honour.

Edward Smith-Stanley, Earl of Derby (1799-1869), born at Knowsley Hall, Prescot, near Liverpool. Conservative Prime Minister in 1852, again from 1858 to 1859, and again from 1866 to 1868.
One of only three Prime Ministers to have served on three separate occasions, though his total time in charge was less than four years. Still the longest serving leader of the Conservative Party.

William Gladstone (1809-98), born in Liverpool. Liberal Prime Minister from 1868 to 1874, again from 1880 to 1885, again in 1886 and again from 1892 to 1894.
The only Prime Minister to serve four separate stints, Gladstone was in charge for 12 years in total and was an MP for 62; only Churchill served as one for longer. He was a significant campaigner on various issues of reform, including Home Rule for Ireland.

David Lloyd George (1863-1945), born in Chorlton-upon-Medlock, Manchester. Liberal Prime Minister from 1916 to 1922.
Although he was born in Lancashire, Lloyd George was, by family and upbringing, more properly a Welshman – and still the only one to serve as Prime Minister. Elected as an MP at 27, he became known as a radical politician for his times, introducing state pensions as Chancellor. He became PM mid-way through the First World War.

BLACKPOOL'S STAR PERFORMERS

Blackpool, and in particular its Winter Gardens complex of theatres, ballrooms and opera houses, has hosted hundreds of famous singers, entertainers, actors and comedians over the years. Here are 30 of the best known.

Arthur Askey	Gracie Fields	Laurel and Hardy
Richard Attenborough	George Formby	Vivien Leigh
Shirley Bassey	Judy Garland	Vera Lynn
The Beatles	John Gielgud	Morecambe and Wise
Sarah Bernhardt	Alec Guinness	John Mills
Charlie Chaplin	Jimi Hendrix	Paul Robeson
Noel Coward	Bob Hope	Frank Sinatra
Bette Davis	Sid James	Tommy Steele
Marlene Dietrich	Tom Jones	Kenneth Williams
Ken Dodd	Lillie Langtree	Norman Wisdom

The vast conference facilities at the complex also make it popular with the leading political parties. The Winter Gardens claims that every British Prime Minister since the Second World War has addressed audiences there at least once.

TEN HISTORIC HOUSES

There are historic houses across Lancashire; here are ten of the most interesting that are open to the public.

Astley Hall, Chorley. Magnificent Elizabethan house, much added to and altered over the centuries and with particularly good ceilings. Owned by Chorley Council since the 1920s and now used as the town's museum and art gallery. Tel 01257 515928 or visit www.chorley.gov.uk.

Brantwood, Coniston. Beautiful house perched above Coniston Water, developed and filled by writer and thinker John Ruskin. Tel 015394 41396 or visit www.brantwood.org.uk.

Gawthorpe Hall, Padiham. One of Lancashire's best Elizabethan houses, built in 1600 for the Shuttleworth family and full of period features. There is a large textiles collection plus important paintings, some showing the hall's connection with the Civil War. Tel 01282 771004 or visit www.nationaltrust.org.uk.

Heaton Hall, near Manchester. Originally built in the 17th century and remodeled in the neo-classical style in the 1770s. The house was given to Manchester's City Council along with its vast park in 1902, and recently underwent restoration. Tel 0161 773 1085 or visit www.heatonpark.org.uk.

Leighton Hall, near Carnforth. Gothic pile that is home to the furniture making Gillow family, with extensive parkland and woodland. Like many of Lancashire's great halls, it is frequently host to TV and film shoots. Tel 01524 734474 or visit www.leightonhall.co.uk.

Lytham Hall, near Lytham. Imposing Georgian manor house, largely built in 1765 on top of a 16th-century house that in turn succeeded a Benedictine priory. It is owned by a local heritage trust and opened up for occasional public tours and private events. Tel 01253 736652 or visit www.lythamhall.org.

Rufford Old Hall, Rufford. Very well preserved timber-framed Tudor house with fine furniture, intricate carvings and extensive collections of tapestry and armour. Tel 01704 821254 or visit www.nationaltrust.org.uk.

Samlesbury Hall, near Preston. Oak timbered medieval house with black and white façade, features including chapel and minstrels' gallery, and extensive gardens. Tel 01254 812010 or visit www.samlesburyhall.co.uk.

Stonyhurst Hall, near Clitheroe. Built in 1592 as a family home, this was given to the Society of Jesus as a new home for their college two centuries later. It continues in the Jesuit tradition as a boarding and day school, with vast buildings and grounds, and visitors are welcome in the summer holidays. Tel 01254 826345 or visit www.stonyhurst.ac.uk.

Towneley Hall, Burnley. Magnificent sprawling house lived in by the Towneley family until they moved out in 1902, taking most of the contents with them. Now owned by the local council, it is home to a museum and art gallery. Tel 01282 424213 or visit www.burnley.gov.uk/towneley.

TREE FACTS

Lancashire has 34,787 acres (14,078 ha) of woodland – equivalent to 54 square miles (140 sq km) or 4.6 per cent of the county's total land area. About half of this woodland is broadleaved, a quarter of it conifer and the rest either mixed, open or felled. Oak and sitka spruce are Lancashire's most common species of broadleaved and conifer respectively.

Increased planting and better forest management has increased the amount of woodland since 1980, when it accounted for 3.7 per cent of Lancashire's land area, but it is still well below the national average of around 12 per cent. County-wide there are 1,244 woods greater than 5 acres (2 ha) in size, and outside woodland there are a further 1.6 million live trees – around 200 per square mile. All these figures were compiled as part of the Forestry Commission's National Inventory of Woodland and Trees, and relate only to the modern administrative county of Lancashire – thus excluding portions of it like mostly urban Merseyside and Greater Manchester and the more rural southern Cumbria.

The largest wooded area in the traditional county of Lancashire is Grizedale Forest, near Hawkshead and Coniston in the Lake District, while the biggest inside the modern county boundaries is Gisburn Forest, in the Forest of Bowland where Lancashire meets Yorkshire. Both are looked after by the Forestry Commission and have lots of walking and cycling trails for visitors. The Commission's four other woodlands in Lancashire are Bidston Moss on the Wirral; Horrocks Woods near Winter Hill; Sutton Manor near St Helens; and Viridor Wood between St Helens and Wigan.

MOUNTAIN RESCUE IN LANCASHIRE

To those who enjoy Lancashire's wild countryside, the county's mountain rescue teams are the fourth emergency service. Whether injured, lost, exhausted or benighted, the teams provide an essential safety net for those who fall foul of the terrain or weather.

Although farmers, shepherds and others in far-flung areas provided an ad hoc rescue service for those in difficulties over the centuries, organised mountain rescue is a relatively modern development. It wasn't until the 1930s that formal rescue strategies began to take shape, and the first civilian rescue team did not launch until after the Second World War in 1947 – based in Coniston, in the southern Lake District and the northernmost part of traditional Lancashire. Other regions began to follow its lead, first in the Lake District and then further south. Besides the teams in the Lake District corner of the county, Lancashire now has three separate units: the Rossendale and Pendle, Bolton, and Bowland Pennine teams, founded in 1962, 1968 and 1980 respectively.

Modern mountain rescue teams are infinitely more skilled and coordinated than their early ancestors. When Coniston's team launched, its kit amounted to a stretcher, some ex-Army blankets, climbing ropes, a lamp and hot water bottles; now, like most teams, it has state of the art medical equipment, offroad vehicles, satellite navigation systems, purpose-built headquarters and training programmes for its members. Because the fells and valleys are much more popular these days, the teams are also busier, between them responding to several hundred call-outs a year across Lancashire – whatever the time of day or night, and whatever the weather. They cover urban as well as rural areas, and are often called on to help trace missing, vulnerable people.

What hasn't changed, however, is the teams' entirely voluntary and charitable status. All members give their time and expertise for free, often out of love for the area they serve, and rely on donations from the public to pay for their equipment and facilities. Much of the money comes from walkers they have previously rescued, who have more reason than most to be grateful for the unique skills and dedication of the teams.

THE BATTLEFIELDS OF LANCASHIRE

From Viking confrontations to civil war skirmishes to Jacobite rebellions, Lancashire has seen plenty of bloody battles. While it is not as rich in battlefields as neighbouring Yorkshire and has few modern-day reminders of the events that took place there, each of the sieges, skirmishes and battles tells a small part of the history of the county and the country. Here are the major encounters on Lancastrian soil over the course of more than a thousand years.

Battle of Whalley, 798. A major battle between the Vikings and Northumberland forces around the River Ribble near Clitheroe in which many, including Alric, were slain.

Siege of Hoghton Tower, 1643. A brief but explosive Civil War siege of this Royalist-held castle between Preston and Blackburn ended with the Parliamentarians accidentally setting off their gunpowder, killing many. The Tower is open to the public for tours and also hosts weddings, film shoots and corporate events.

Siege of Thurland Castle, 1643. A series of minor sieges over four months ended with Parliamentarians flushing out Royalist men. The castle, near Tunstall, has now been developed into luxury apartments. Around the same time there was a similar **Siege of Hornby Castle**, a few miles south. The castle is now privately owned.

Siege of Lathom House, 1644-5. Another siege of a Royalist stronghold, this time by several thousand Parliamentarians. The house near Ormskirk was well fortified and held for months before it was surrendered in late 1645. It was later destroyed, though a new Lathom House took its place.

The Storming of Bolton, 1644. Royalist forces from Lathom House joined this attack by Royalist commander and King Charles I's nephew Prince Rupert on the town of Bolton, killing at least a thousand. A week later, Rupert's men went south to overcome brief Parliamentarian resistance at the **Siege of Liverpool**.

First Battle of Preston, 1648. A key battle in the Second Civil War, in which a Scottish army travelling south in support of King Charles I was defeated by the Parliamentarians on Ribbleton Moor. Preston's Harris Museum has material on the battle.

Battle of Winwick Pass, 1648. Surviving Royalist and Scottish forces we re finished off soon after Preston in this brutal battle near Warrington. Oliver Cromwell's Parliamentarians claimed a thousand dead and double that number captured.

Second Battle of Preston, 1715. One of the last battles fought on English soil, between the Jacobites and government forces. Savage fighting in the town and around the River Ribble ended in defeat for the Jacobites.

Although not technically a battle, Lancashire's list is added to by the **Peterloo Massacre** or the **Encounter of St Peter's Fields**. Here, in August 1819, a gathering of around 60,000 people campaigning for universal suffrage and other reforms was brutally broken up by government cavalry, who killed at least 15 and wounded hundreds.

It is sometimes called the Battle of Peterloo in ironic reference to the Battle of Waterloo four years earlier. St Peter's Square in Manchester has a plaque marking the event, though a campaign is ongoing for a more substantial commemoration.

LANCASHIRE'S COAT OF ARMS

The official coat of arms of the modern administrative county of Lancashire incorporates three emblems of the famous red rose on a gold shield. To either side are lions standing on their hind legs with forepaws on the shield, while above on the crest is another lion on all fours on a golden wreath. Emblazoned underneath is Lancashire's official motto – *In Concilio Consilium*. Critics of some of the council's decisions over the years may consider its loose translation – 'In Council is Wisdom' – to be a little immodest.

An alternative Lancashire coat of arms, designed by scurrilous folk over the border in Yorkshire, presents a rather different view of the county. Its design incorporates the common Lancastrian clichés of a pair of clogs and a jug of ale, together with a bug (like Lancastrians, in their view, a nuisance) and an owl (because they are fond of the dark, apparently). The design was a riposte to a similar joke by Lancastrians, who gave their friends across the Pennines a coat of arms that included motifs of a fly (because it, like Yorkshiremen, will drink with anyone) and a magpie (because it talks endlessly).

LANCASHIRE FOOD – BLACK PUDDING

Lancashire is not the only county claiming rights to the black pudding, but the red rose county does proudly call itself home to the original and best examples of this distinctive food.

Blood sausages like black pudding are thought to date back to Greek or Roman times, when rudimentary versions were eaten for their nutritional value and to make the most of every last bit of slaughtered animals. The sausages as we know them probably spread across England with monks from Europe, where many countries still have their own popular versions of the delicacy. They evolved and remained particularly popular in Lancashire, where competition among specialist producers is now fierce, each convinced that their particular secret recipe is the best. The black pudding's headquarters is Bury, home to dozens of producers in the late 19th century and still the place to find several, especially at the town's market.

Specialist producers thrive because making black pudding at home is not easily done – even if you have the stomach for it. Pigs' blood is difficult to obtain unless you have animals of your own to take to an abattoir, so most people prefer to buy their black pudding in cooked rings, ready to be sliced up and reheated, gently so it doesn't break up. The pudding is originally cooked with a range of filler ingredients like pork fat, oatmeal, onions and bread, plus seasonings that often include pepper, mace or coriander. Cooked until the point at which it solidifies on cooling, the mixture is then pushed into casings, much as a sausage is prepared, and then boiled up for another ten minutes or so.

Black pudding has long had a reputation as a cheap and rustic food, most commonly eaten as part of a fry-up breakfast. But it is much more versatile than that and is now enjoying something of a renaissance, appearing on the menus of upmarket restaurants across Lancashire, and often paired with pork, lamb or fish.

Blackpudding's popularity is such that Lancashire even has a sporting event dedicated to the delicacy: the World Black Pudding Throwing Championships. Held each year in Ramsbottom near Manchester, the event's organisers set up a stack of Yorkshire puddings and invite participants to knock as many of them down as possible with a throw of a black pudding, wrapped up in ladies' tights to stop it disintegrating. As a sporting discipline it's probably one of the least prestigious in which to be called a world champion, but as food fights go it's pretty spectacular – and it certainly reinforces Lancastrians' feelings of superiority over their Yorkshire counterparts.

A recipe using black pudding

100 g (half a ring) of black pudding
8 scallops
1 red onion, finely sliced
1 tbsp unsalted butter
Salt and freshly ground black pepper
Olive oil
Water

Gently fry the sliced red onion in a little olive oil until it is caramelised. Put a heavy frying pan on a low heat and add roughly half the butter. Slice the black pudding into eight even rounds, and once the butter has melted, add them to the pan. Leave for a few minutes on the same gentle heat and turn. When they are warmed through, remove and keep warm.

Turn the heat under the pan up to high, and when it is very hot add the rest of the butter with a drop of olive oil to stop it burning. Season the scallops on both sides with salt and pepper, add them to the pan and sear for a minute and a half on each side, only moving them to flip them over. Remove and place four scallops on top of four slices of black pudding on each of two plates. Now add a couple of tablespoons of water to the caramelised red onion and turn up the heat to quickly boil and reduce slightly. Drizzle this over the scallops and black pudding. Serve with salad leaves for a starter, or mashed potato for a more substantial supper.

GREAT LANCASTRIANS – ROBERT PEEL

Perhaps with William Gladstone and David Lloyd George, Sir Robert Peel is the most significant of all the politicians to have been born in Lancashire. Prime Minister for more than five years over two terms, he was born into immense wealth yet became a committed social reformer – a rare combination in 19th-century British politics.

Peel's father had made much of his money from Lancashire's growing textile industry, and lived at Bury when Robert was born in 1788. After he was educated at Harrow and Oxford University, his father's influence and money bought him a Tory seat in parliament at the age of just 21. He cut his teeth in politics as Under-Secretary for War and the colonies and then Chief Secretary for Ireland, but it was as Home Secretary from 1822 that he first made his mark. Embarking on a major overhaul of criminal law and prisons, he cut the number of crimes that were punishable by death and improved conditions and education for inmates. In 1829 he created the London Metropolitan Police, the first organised police force in the world and an idea that soon spread around UK cities and the world. Peelers and bobbies are both nicknames for policemen that derive from his name.

After several years in opposition when the Tory government fell in 1830, Peel was asked by King William IV to become Prime Minister, though he resigned a year later after being frustrated by his party's inability to get acts through parliament. Returning again in 1841, he now embarked on his second great phase of reform. First came the Mines Act, which put an end to women and children working underground, and then the Factory Act, which limited the hours they could work in factories and raised safety standards. His reforms had a particular impact in his home county, where women and very young children had previously toiled in virtual slavery in the mills, weaving sheds and factories. At a time when many in Britain were out of work, Peel also took steps to improve international trade and economic recovery.

In 1845 Peel turned to repealing the Corn Laws, which had been brought in to protect British agriculture but which led to huge suffering when harvests failed, especially in Ireland. Despite opposition from landowners and fellow Tories, Peel insisted that foreign grain be allowed in to ease the famine, and after months of debate he eventually gathered enough support to force his repeal through. Later the same day, his party split over the issue and weakened, Peel was defeated on another bill and soon resigned. He never held office again, and died four years later, after falling from his horse in London.

It is easy to over-estimate the scale of Peel's reform – conditions for many workers remained dreadful, and some historians argue that his changes were politically rather than socially motivated. But it is a measure of his commitment to social justice that on several occasions Peel put his humanitarian principles before his party, aware that his measures would cripple his own leadership. His popularity among the British working and middle classes was confirmed by the large sums of money raised from public subscriptions for a statue in Manchester and a Peel Tower on Holcombe Hill near Bury after his death. Here, as in several other British towns, there is also a pub named in his honour, and Bury's football club remains almost certainly the only one in England to have a mascot inspired by a politician – Robbie the Bobbie.

FOUR HUNDRED YEARS OF EXTREME WEATHER

Although Lancashire's reputation for an unwelcoming climate is largely undeserved, it has probably had more than its fair share of extreme weather over the years. Here are some of the more noteworthy meteorological happenings over the last four centuries.

1616 The legendary 'Lambard's Flood' decimates much of Manchester

1662 Hailstones 'as big as ordinary apples' fall on Ormskirk, according to the diary of a local vicar. 'All except the ignorant were much terrified, thinking it had been the Day of Judgment.'

1776 Vibrations from an earthquake in Manchester are so strong that church bells are set ringing around the town

1802 Gale force winds snuff out gas lamps in the larger towns and topple masonry, killing several people

1823 The lower slopes of the Pennines are covered in snow in June

1839 A hurricane wrecks several Lancashire ports, sinking or driving ashore dozens of ships

1866 A flood swamps Manchester and Salford after the River Irwell bursts its banks

1880 Old Trafford in Manchester establishes its reputation as cricket's soggiest ground after a entire Test match is lost to rain for the first time

1893 Preston gets 1.25 inches (32 mm) of rain in five minutes in August – still a national record

1903 A train on the Furness Railway derails as storms sweep much of Lancashire

1939 The coldest Christmas in decades sees parts of the Mersey covered with ice

1940 Several days of smog coat Manchester; the effects are so foul that locals suspect German chemical warfare

1946 One of the harshest winters on record results in snow lying on the ground in Lancashire virtually continuously from December to March

1963 Another fiercely cold winter freezes lakes and canals across the county

1964 Hailstones the size of golf balls rain down on several East Lancashire towns

1972 A minor earthquake topples chimneys in Accrington, Leyland and Rawtenstall

1976 The summer, one of the hottest on record, brings less than 0.4 inches (10 mm) of rain in many towns in August

1982 The coldest January for a century freezes parts of the Mersey and the sea at Southport

THE CENTRE OF BRITAIN

Lancastrians like to believe that Britain revolves around their county – and they may be right. The village of Dunsop Bridge in the Forest of Bowland lays claim to being the centre of gravity of the British Isles – the point at which a flat cut-out of the country would balance on a pinhead. The exact spot, calculated by the Ordnance Survey, is on a peat bog on Brennand Farm a few miles north of the village.

But since determining a country's centre can be done in other ways, like working out the mid-point of its line of longitude, other places rival Dunsop Bridge for Britain's title. Among these is the town of Haltwhistle in Northumberland, which boasts about its claim on signs and banners around the town. Dunsop Bridge is much more modest, with only a small plaque near a telephone box commemorating the village's pivotal importance.

LANCASHIRE ON FILM

Lancashire has long been a popular location for film-makers, and it continues to market itself heavily to UK and US studios as a versatile setting for all sorts of movies. Here are 20 popular films to have been set or filmed at least partly in the county's cities, towns and countryside.

Brief Encounter (1945). The film's most famous scenes were shot at Carnforth Station, and fans of the film still visit in their droves.

Hobson's Choice (1954). Non-studio scenes were filmed in Salford.

The Entertainer (1960). Shot in both Blackpool and Morecambe.

Whistle Down the Wind (1961). Filmed in Downham, near Clitheroe.

A Kind of Loving (1962). Classic Alan Bates movie, shot in Lancashire locations including Bolton, Manchester and Preston.

Yanks (1979). Wartime drama shot in various spots around Manchester.

Chariots of Fire (1981). Scenes set in the British Embassy in Paris were filmed at Liverpool town hall.

Monty Python's The Meaning of Life (1983). Features scenes shot in Colne.

A Private Function (1984). Scenes shot in Barnoldswick.

The Hunt for Red October (1990). Some scenes filmed in Liverpool.

Richard III (1995). Modern update of Shakespeare's play, featuring scenes shot in Carnforth.

Whatever Happened to Harold Smith? (1999). Shot on Blackpool Pleasure Beach.

There's Only One Jimmy Grimble (2000). School scenes shot in Hulme and Ormskirk and stadium scenes at Maine Road in Manchester.

The 51st State (2001). Filmed largely on location in Liverpool and Manchester.

The Parole Officer (2001). Largely shot on location in Lancashire, including Manchester, Liverpool and Blackpool.

24 Hour Party People (2002). Film about Manchester's music scene, largely shot in the city.

Possession (2002). Scenes shot at Leighton Hall near Carnforth.

Alfie (2004). Liverpool and Manchester both doubled for New York in this remake of the classic film.

Frozen (2005). Drama set around Morecambe Bay and filmed in and around Fleetwood.

Miss Potter (2006). Various southern Lake District locations featured in this biopic of Beatrix Potter, many of them around Coniston Water.

THE FOUR CORNERS OF LANCASHIRE

It is a sign of how much Lancashire's traditional boundaries have been toyed with that none of the most northerly, southerly, easterly or westerly points now lie inside the modern-day administrative borders.

Two of the four extreme points of the ceremonial county are both now part of the administrative county of Cumbria. The village of Hawkshead in the Lake District National Park is the northernmost settlement, lying just above Coniston. And the westernmost point is Barrow-in-Furness or, more precisely, the adjunct area of Vickerstown on the Isle of Walney, built to accommodate workers at Barrow.

About 100 miles (161 km) from Hawkshead, the southern tip of Lancashire lies in the village of Hale, 10 miles (16 km) southeast of the centre of Liverpool and 4 miles (6 km) southwest of Widnes. After the rejigging of county boundaries, it was placed in the far reaches of Cheshire for administrative purposes. The easternmost settlement wholly in Lancashire is Littleborough near Rochdale, now part of Greater Manchester. Another town on roughly the same line of longitude, Todmorden, is divided into Lancashire and Yorkshire by the traditional county boundary, the River Calder, while another, Laneshaw Bridge near Colne, lies almost as far east and remains wholly part of Lancashire.

AREAS OF OUTSTANDING NATURAL BEAUTY

Lancashire has two of England's 35 Areas of Outstanding Natural Beauty – landscapes that are so distinctive and important that they deserve special measures to safeguard them. They are:

Arnside and Silverside

Limestone hills, ancient woodlands and the shores of Morecambe Bay characterise this small, 29 square mile (75 sq km) site along the border of Lancashire and Cumbria. It's a popular spot for walkers and wildlife lovers in particular.

Forest of Bowland

Forest here refers to the area's past as a royal hunting ground rather than its trees, and much of this 312 square mile (808 sq km) site is a wilderness of heather moorland, bogs and green valleys, dotted with farms and small villages. Fells in the area include Pendle Hill, famous for its associations with witchcraft and the birth of the Quaker movement.

LANCASHIRE'S NATIONAL PARK

Despite its large expanses of natural beauty, Lancashire's modern boundaries contain none of Britain's 15 National Parks. Measured by its traditional borders, however, its northernmost section takes in the southwest corner of the Lake District National Park.

Designated in 1951, the park covers 885 square miles (2,292 sq km), of which perhaps a quarter falls into traditional Lancashire. That portion includes the popular tourist towns of Hawkshead and Coniston, and two of the Lake District's 18 lakes, Coniston Water and Windermere. Here are some more figures about the Lake District National Park:

41,831 . . . . permanent residents

17,937 . . . . household spaces

5,724 . . . . miles (9,212 km) of watercourses

2,225 . . . . miles (3,580 km) of public footpaths and bridleways

3,210 . . . height in feet (978 m) of the highest mountain, Scafell Pike

1,740 . . . . listed buildings

275 . . . . scheduled monuments

132 . . . . sites of special scientific interest

80 . . . . parishes

47 . . . . residents per square mile

40 . . . . miles (64 km) length from north to south

33 . . . . miles (53 km) width from east to west

23 . . . . square miles (60 sq km) of still water in the lakes

21 . . . . conservation areas

10.5 . . . . length in miles (17 km) of the longest lake, Windermere

9 . . . . registered parks and gardens of historic interest

8 . . . . national nature reserves

3 . . . . settlements with a population of more than 3,000
(Windermere / Bowness, Keswick and Ambleside)

THE FLAT CAP

No item of clothing has identified Lancastrian men or their Yorkshire counterparts quite so readily over the centuries as the flat cap – and although it is more rarely seen these days, it remains a powerful emblem of the working class north.

The classic flat cap is usually made from tweed or wool, with a little brim at the front and a higher peak at the back. Its use may date back as far as the 15th century, but it undoubtedly had its heyday in the industrial England of the 19th and early 20th centuries, when it was hugely popular among workers in Lancashire's mills, mines and factories. Photos of workplaces and leisure activities of the period invariably depict a sea of caps on the heads of just about every man and boy.

The flat cap was never the sole preserve of either the north or the working class – it was worn across Britain, and sported by the landed gentry at play, too – but along with symbols like clogs, whippets and racing pigeons the association has stuck, and it has become something of a stereotype of the county. The dozens of hat manufacturers that once served the Lancashire market are now long gone, replaced by cheaper manufacturing centres in far-flung corners of the developing world, but the cap has enjoyed something of a renaissance in the last few years. Sported by celebrities and featured in famous designers' collections, it has become popular among young urban types in particular. To many rural Lancastrians like farmers, however, its no-nonsense coverage and warmth never went out of fashion.

LANCASHIRE'S TOP TOURIST ATTRACTIONS

Although it is more usually associated with the Lake District these days, the shores of Windermere actually form part of the northern boundary of what is often called 'proper' Lancashire. The lake is also home to the county's most popular tourist attraction – Windermere Lake Cruises. Hosting nearly 1.2 million customers in 2008, the lake's ferries are also the fourth most popular paid-for attraction in England. Two more Lancashire attractions, Liverpool's Tate Gallery and Maritime Museum, also attracted more than 1 million visitors in 2008, and like many of the museums and galleries on this list, their numbers have swelled in recent years by virtue of their free admission. Liverpool, in fact, is home to six of the ten leading attractions.

This list of top tourist attractions is based on research by the VisitEngland agency. Some caution is required, as not all attractions are willing or able to supply visitor numbers, and the list is therefore missing obviously popular attractions like Blackpool Pleasure Beach. With that caveat, VisitEngland's top ten attractions in Lancashire are:

Attraction	Visitors in 2008
1 Windermere Lake Cruises, Bowness	1,199,216
2 Tate Liverpool	1,088,504
3 Merseyside Maritime Museum	1,020,712
4 Liverpool Museum	787,767
5 Manchester Art Gallery	462,166
6 International Slavery Museum, Liverpool	414,480
7 Walker Art Gallery, Liverpool	396,356
8 Metropolitan Cathedral of Christ the King, Liverpool	364,347
9 Blackpool Zoo	337,000
10 Cuerden Valley Park	275,000

A CALENDAR OF TRADITIONS

Like most counties of England, Lancashire is steeped in customs, festivals and celebrations that are observed year in, year out. Here are nine of the most interesting and popular annual traditions, some of them dating back centuries.

Pace Egging and Plays, Easter

Once popular across England, pace egging endures most strongly in Lancashire and Yorkshire. Derived from the Latin *pasch* meaning Easter, pace eggs are eggs decorated especially for the occasion, then either eaten or given to pace eggers, who would walk in procession through towns and villages. Pace egg plays celebrate the arrival of spring and consequent rebirth, dramatised by an actor dressed as St George slaying various villains symbolising winter. The tradition thrives in Bury and surrounding towns and villages, where pace eggers perform on the weekend before Easter, as well as in several towns and villages on the Furness peninsula. Pace egg rolling meanwhile takes place on hills in Bury, Preston and Ulverston on Good Friday, Easter Sunday and Easter Monday respectively.

Bacup Coconutters Dance, Easter Saturday
An odd annual event in which the Britannia Coconut Dancers blacken their faces and don an eccentric ensemble of dark jumper, white sash, black clogs and red, white and blue kilt to dance around the old mill town, accompanied by a marching band. They have round pieces of wood – the 'coconuts' – on their hands, waist and knees to make a rhythmic sound as they go, and are marshalled by a 'whipper-in'. The origins of the event are uncertain – some see unsettling connotations with the custom of blackface minstrelsy, but others link the dancers' appearance to a tradition of disguising oneself from evil spirits, or even local coal mining.

The Black Knight of Ashton, Easter Monday
Another eccentric tradition whereby an effigy of a black knight – sometimes called the black lad – was carried around the town of Ashton-under-Lyne on a horse and jeered at by crowds before being taken down and pelted with mud and stones. The knight is supposed to represent a tyrannical 15th-century lord of the manor, though there is little historical evidence for this. After degenerating into a rather violent and drunken occasion, the tradition was first suspended and then refined into a more civilised general pageant. It died out again in the 1950s but has recently been revived as a festival for the town.

Whit Walks, Whit Friday or Sunday
The tradition of the Whit Walks – church-organised processions through local towns, accompanied by bands and followed by great merriment – was once popular across Lancashire and Yorkshire. It involved Sunday School children in particular, dressed up in new clothes and led by a May or Rose queen and her attendants. Although the walks have declined in popularity, they are still followed in plenty of places, including Manchester, Ashton-under-Lyne and Mossley.

Brass Band Contests, Whit Friday
An annual celebration of brass music, in which dozens of bands play at various spots between Oldham in Lancashire and Saddleworth in Yorkshire. Assessed by judges, they then move on to the next contest before an overall winner is decided. The location on the border between the red and white rose counties encourages fierce cross-Pennine competition in particular, though bands now come from far afield. The event grew out of the annual Whit Walk here.

Warrington Walking Day, early July
A Whit Walk-style parade that sees churches, Scouts and other local organisations march through the town with banners, accompanied by

bands. The day was first organised by a local vicar as a more wholesome form of entertainment than rival attractions such as horse racing, and was first held in the 1830s, though it wasn't until nearly a century later that various Christian denominations agreed to march together on the same route. It is held on the Friday nearest to 1 July and still attracts thousands of participants.

Preston Guild, late August and early September

Staged every 20 years, the Preston Guild is a major event in the city. It dates back to the 12th century, when a charter was granted to Preston's guild – a group of merchants who met occasionally to admit new members and celebrate their achievements with banquets and entertainments. The guild has long since lost its powers and responsibilities, but the tradition of a city-wide party continues. The first guild of the 21st century falls in 2012. The phrase 'once every Preston Guild' is sometimes used in Lancashire to describe something that doesn't happen very often.

Urswick Rushbearing, late September

Rushbearing dates from the times when churches had mud floors covered with rushes that were changed once a year amid great ceremony and celebration. The tradition died out in many places when floors became paved, but it continues to be marked in several places including Urswick on the Furness peninsula of Lancashire. Local children carry the rushes through the town to St Mary and St Michael's Church, accompanied by a band and clergy and led by a rushbearing queen. It takes place on the Sunday nearest to St Michael's Day, 29 September.

Mischief Night, 31 October or 4 November

This tradition has died out in most places, but it perseveres in some Lancashire towns. It began as a day on which children could play tricks on their elders without fear of punishment, but has lately become more of an excuse for a night of vandalism that keeps police on their toes.

LANCASHIRE INDUSTRY – COAL

Coal mining in Britain has always been more a way of life than a job. In Lancashire, it dominated large sections of the county for decades, the mines providing work for generations of families and shaping their nearby towns and villages. Now, for better or worse, the industry has gone – but it remains a part of a history of which many Lancastrians are fiercely proud.

From the 16th century until the Industrial Revolution, mining here had been small-scale, a few shallow pits first turning out enough coal for local people's needs, then producing extra for transport further afield. As the country industrialised, however, it expanded into a vast enterprise, the soaring demand opening up new pits and sending miners deeper and deeper underground in search of more coal. Lancashire's cotton mills were particularly thirsty for fuel, and at one time the county's coalfield was the most prolific in Britain, stretching some 500 square miles (1,295 sq km) from Burnley in the north to the fringes of Manchester in the southeast and Ormskirk in the west. The three hundred or so collieries were mostly small, but they employed tens of thousands of men and boys between them.

After the First World War, recovery of coal by hand was gradually succeeded by machine mining, and pit ponies by mechanical haulage. It made the miners' work slightly easier, but it remained a backbreaking job, carried out over long shifts in cramped, filthy conditions and extremes of hot and cold.

The work was fearsomely dangerous, too. Many thousands of people died in Lancashire's mines, from underground fires, floods, accidents and, most common of all, explosions. The worst of them occurred at a pit at the Hulton Colliery at Westhoughton between Wigan and Bolton, known locally as the Pretoria Pit, in 1910. A build-up of gas was ignited by a faulty lamp and led to an explosion that killed 344 people, including many men and boys from the same families. Major disasters continued until the 1960s, when safety regulations and techniques finally helped to reduce the dreadful risk.

By this time the industry had been nationalised and Lancashire's mines had fallen to around 40, the rest having been exhausted of their coal or proved uneconomical. When the government tried to merge or close many of the remaining pits in 1984, it prompted protests that led to Lancashire's several thousand miners going out on strike. The area was moderate compared to the northeast, where clashes between the miners and police turned more violent, but the strike nevertheless caused enormous hardship for those who joined it, and tension for those who eventually broke it by going back to work. After the strike was finally wound down the next year, Lancashire's remaining mines did not last long. The last of the county's pits to close was Parkside Colliery at Newton-le-Willows in 1993, and although coal reserves remain, there is now no deep mining anywhere in the county.

The jolt of closures was not as great in Lancashire as it was in counties like Yorkshire and Durham, where there were many more pits, but the end of mining has undoubtedly left a scar on the coalfield region. Some of the towns that turned out generations of miners have built other industries to replace coal, but the sense of anger over the decline of the industry is still keenly felt elsewhere.

The best place to learn more about Lancashire's mining heritage is the Astley Green Colliery Museum in a village just east of Leigh. The only colliery in the area to have survived demolition, it was preserved after is closure in 1970 by the council and a group of enthusiasts. It now opens on a few afternoons a week to display its collection of mining equipment and memorabilia (tel 01942 828121 or visit www.agcm.org.uk for times). Another poignant reminder of the coal era is the male voice choir at Parkside, still going strong long after the end of the mine that brought its members together.

LANCASHIRE'S 14 DISTRICTS

The complicated and controversial reorganisation of county boundaries in 1974, plus subsequent government rejigging, has left the modern administrative county of Lancashire with 14 districts. Together with their administrative headquarters, they are:

Blackburn with Darwen (Blackburn)

Blackpool (Blackpool)

Burnley (Burnley)

Chorley (Chorley)

Fylde (Lytham St Annes)

Hyndburn (Accrington)

Lancaster (Lancaster)

Pendle (Nelson)

Preston (Preston)

Ribble Valley (Clitheroe)

Rossendale (Rawtenstall)

South Ribble (Leyland)

West Lancashire (Ormskirk)

Wyre (Poulton-le-Fylde)

GREAT LANCASHIRE INVENTIONS

Lancashire has been home to plenty of the country's great inventors over the years, most notably during the Industrial Revolution. From the pioneering to the peculiar, here are a dozen of the county's most interesting inventions.

James Bullough of Accrington was, with William Kenworthy, the inventor of the **Lancashire loom**, a power loom that helped make the county England's weaving centre. He worked for some time in Blackburn, but was driven out by workers who thought – correctly as it turned out – that his design would put them out of a job.

As the chief designer for aircraft manufacturer Avro between the two world wars, Roy Chadwick, born in Farnworth, designed more than two hundred planes including the famous **Lancaster Bomber**. He died in one of his planes that had been wrongly serviced.

Bolton-born Samuel Crompton built on the work of other Industrial Revolution pioneers to create a new machine that further revolutionised cotton in Lancashire: the **spinning mule**, named because it was a hybrid of Richard Arkwright's spinning frame and the spinning jenny (see below).

Thomas Edmondson, a Lancaster-born station master, designed the **Edmondson Railway Ticket** – the small piece of cardboard carrying details of passengers' journeys that became the standard ticket across the growing rail network from the 1840s.

By picking up the ball and running with it when he should have been kicking it, Salford-born William Webb Ellis is widely credited with inventing the sport of **rugby**, though the story may be apocryphal.

By day George Garrett was a clergyman in his home city of Manchester, but in his spare time he designed the world's first **mechanically driven submarine**. Like many inventions it was somewhat flawed, and his early subs were both unstable and unbearably hot inside.

Born at Stanhill and living in Blackburn, James Hargreaves invented the **spinning jenny** in 1764. The device made it much easier for workers to produce yarn, making Hargreaves, with Arkwright, chief among the pioneers of the Industrial Revolution.

Eric Laithwaite, born in Atherton, designed the world's first ever **magnetically levitating train** – the MagLev. After initial interest the government pulled out of a project in the UK, but Laithwaite's invention was adopted elsewhere.

John Mercer was a Great Harwood-born textile chemist who invented a process to give materials like cotton a lustrous, silky finish by treating it with a caustic solution. It was refined after his death and given the name of **mercerisation** in his honour.

Among many other achievements in paleontology, Lancaster-born Richard Owen coined the word **dinosaur**, from the Greek words *deinos* (terrible and powerful) and *sauros* (lizard). He was also one of the founders of the Natural History Museum in London.

James Sumner was born in Leyland and went on to found the motor firm that took the town's name. Fascinated by motorised transport, he designed a mechanised tricycle before inventing the slightly more practical **steam-powered lawnmower**.

Thomas Wilkinson, born in Ormskirk and a vicar at Kirkby in Liverpool, invented the **gold balances**, weighing scales for gold. Kirkby has a pub called the Gold Balance named after him.

LANCASHIRE POEMS – 'BOWTON'S YARD'

Although he was born in Yorkshire and lived for much of his life in Cheshire, there are few better chroniclers of life in 19th-century industrial Lancashire than Samuel Laycock. Born in 1826, he worked in a cotton mill from the age of just nine, and started writing poems in the 1850s. He became known as a people's poet, his work full of everyday working class experiences that were told without artifice in authentic Lancashire dialect and intended to be sung as well as read. Suffering from ill health, he later moved to the Lancashire coast, where he died in 1897.

'Bowton's Yard', one of his most famous poems, is about a courtyard of grim workers' houses in Stalybridge on the Lancashire-Cheshire border. The yard was pulled down in the 1960s, leaving the poem as a memorial to a vanished way of life in the old cotton towns. Full of close observation, humour and affection, it has been credited by Tony Warren, the creator of *Coronation Street*, as one of the inspirations for his famous soap.

> At number one i' Bowton's yard, mi gronny keeps a skoo,
> But hasn't mony scholars yet, hoo's only one or two;
> They sen th' owd woman's rather cross – well, well, it may be so;
> Aw know hoo box'd me rarely once, an' pood mi ears an' o.

> At number two lives widow Burns, hoo weshes clooas for folk,
> Their Billy, that's her son, gets jobs at wheelin' coke;
> They sen hoo coarts wi' Sam-o'-Neds, 'at lives at number three;
> It may be so, aw conno tell, it matters nowt to me.

> At number three, reet facin' th' pump, Ned Grimshaw keeps a shop;
> He's Eccles Cakes, an' gingerbread, an' treacle beer, an' pop;
> He sells oat-cakes an' o, does Ned, he has boath soft an' hard,
> An' everybody buys off him 'at lives i' Bowton's yard.

> At number four Jack Blunderick lives; he goes to th' mill an' weayves;
> An' then, at th' week-end, when he's time, he pows a bit an' shaves;
> He's badly off, is Jack, poor lad; he's rayther lawm, they sen,
> An' his childer keep him deawn a bit – aw think they'n nine or ten.

> At number five aw live mysel', wi' owd Susannah Grimes,
> But dunno loike so very weel – hoo turns me eawt sometimes;
> An' when awm in there's ne'er no leet, aw have to ceawer i' th' dark;
> Aw conno pay mi lodgin' brass, because awm eawt o' wark.

> At number six, next dur to us, an' close o' th' side o' th' speawt,
> Owd Susie Collins sells mo' drink, but hoo's welly allus abeawt;
> But heaw it is that is the case awm sure aw conno tell,
> Hoo happen maks it very sweet, an' sups it o hersel!

> At number seven there's nob'dy lives, they left it yesterday,
> Th' bum-baylis coom an' mark'd their things, and took 'em o away;
> They took 'em in a donkey-cart – aw know newt wheer they went –
> Aw reckon they'n bin ta'en and sowd because they owed some rent.

> At number eight – they're Yawshur folk – there's only th' mon an' woife,
> Aw think aw ne'er seed nicer folk nor these i' o mi life;
> Yo'll never yer 'em foin' eawt, loike lots o' married folk,
> They allus seem good-tempered like, an' ready wi' a joke.

At number nine th' owd cobbler lives – th' owd chap 'at mends
my shoon,
He's getting very weak an' done, he'll ha' to leov us soon;
He reads his Bible every day, an' sings just loike a lark,
He says he's practisin' for heaven – he's welly done his wark.

At number ten James Bowton lives – he's th' noicest heawse i' th' row;
He's allus plenty o' sum'at t' eat, an lots o' brass an' o;
An' when he rides an' walks abeawt he's dress'd up very fine,
But he isn't hawve as near to heaven as him at number nine.

At number 'leven mi uncle lives – aw co him uncle Tum,
He goes to concerts, up an' deawn, an' plays a kettle-drurn;
I' bands o' music, an' sich things, he seems to tak' a pride,
An' allus maks as big a noise as o i' th' place beside.

At number twelve, an' th' end o' th' row, Joe Stiggins deals i' ale;
He's sixpenny, an' fourpenny, dark-coloured, an' he's pale;
But aw ne'er touch it, for aw know it's ruined mony a bard –
Awm th' only chap as doesn't drink 'at lives i' Bowton's yard.

An' neaw awve dune aw'll say good-bye, an' leave yo' for awhile;
Aw know aw haven't towd mi tale i' sich a first-rate style;
But iv yo're pleased awm satisfied, an' ax for no reward
For tellin' who mi nayburs are 'at live i' Bowton's Yard.

Glossary: *gronny* (line 1) means granny; *skoo* (1) means school; *boo* (2)
means she; *pood* (4) means pulled; *o* (4) means all; *wheelin' coke* (6)
means transporting coal; *sen* (7) means say; *pows* (14) means pours or
drinks; *lawm* (15) means lame; *ceawer* (19) means shower; *speawt* (21)
means spout; *bum-baylis* (26) means bum-bailiffs; *Yawshur* (29) means
Yorkshire; *foin' eawt* (31) means falling out; *shoon* (33) means shoes;
welly done his wark (36) means really done his work.

SHAKESPEARE IN LANCASHIRE

Lancashire has produced many fine writers over the years, and it may well
have helped to shape the most famous one of all: William Shakespeare.

Very little is known of Shakespeare's life before his late twenties,
and efforts to piece together his 'lost' years are fraught with difficulty.
But a case has been growing among scholars that from his late teens

until his arrival in London in his late twenties, he may have spent several years in Lancashire at two of its famous ancestral houses.

Shakespeare's journey here would certainly make sense if, as is now commonly claimed, Shakespeare was a Catholic. At a time of widespread suspicion of the religion, Lancashire was a stronghold for Catholicism and a relatively safe haven for its followers. Whether Shakespeare left his home town of Stratford because of the threat of persecution or simply to secure work will probably never be known, but what is now fairly clear is that he stayed for some time at Hoghton Tower near Preston. The Hoghtons were known to have taken in other Catholics, and Shakespeare may well have been given shelter here in return for duties like teaching at the house. He would have been able to soak up knowledge and writing influences from books in the house's library, perhaps joining in the performances of theatrical or musical works in the banqueting hall too.

One of the few undisputed facts in the story is that Alexander Hoghton's will made provision for a 'William Shakeshafte', who – in an age when surnames were flexible and often disguised, in this case to avoid detection as a Catholic – could well have been Shakespeare. On his death, he was to be looked after by Hoghton's friend Thomas Hesketh, than at Rufford Old Hall, 15 miles (24 km) southwest of Hoghton. Hoghton also bequeathed to Hesketh his 'instruments and play clothes', so it is likely that Shakespeare continued his performing in Rufford's great hall, and possibly further afield with local groups. Some scholars detect aspects of the countryside around Hoghton Tower and Rufford Old Hall in some of Shakespeare's plays, though separating these from other influences in his work is very difficult. More likely is that Shakespeare arrived in London with one of the theatrical troupes with which he performed in Lancashire, thus starting his career as a playwright as well as an actor.

A second literary claim to fame for Hoghton Tower is that it was visited nearly three centuries after Shakespeare by Charles Dickens, while on a tour of the region to research, among other things, his novel *Hard Times*. The house was very run-down at the time of his visit in 1854, and his stay there inspired Dickens to write a melancholy short story, *George Silverman's Explanation*. Hoghton was largely restored soon afterwards, and it is now open to day visitors from July to September and on Bank Holiday weekends. Rufford Old Hall is owned by the National Trust and opened to the public between March and October. Both places occasionally host performances of plays by Shakespeare and others.

ENGLAND'S SMALLEST STREET

As well as being recognised by English Heritage as the best preserved of all of England's old cotton towns, Bacup in Rossendale can lay claim to the smallest street in England. Measuring about 17 feet (5 m) from end to end, Elgin Street is home to just one building entrance and dates back to the early 19th century. It also held the record for the world's shortest street until 2006 when, to much local disappointment, the town of Wick in Scotland claimed the honour from Guinness World Records for Ebenezer Place, which measures less than 7 feet (2 m) and has also housed a single building since it was created in 1887.

TEN PARKS AND GARDENS

Lancashire has dozens of wonderful gardens, some of them part of grand country estates but a surprising number to be found in city or town centres. Here are ten of the county's best, all open to the public at least some of the time.

Avenham Park, Preston. Classic Victorian public park next to the River Ribble, featuring fountains, a Japanese garden and trails. Preston's Miller Park is also excellent. Visit www.avenhampark.com.

Cobble Hey, near Garstang. Peaceful and pretty country garden on a working farm, featuring woodland, ponds, orchards and rockeries and views over the Forest of Bowland. Tel 01995 602643 or visit www.cobblehey.co.uk.

Cuerden Valley Park, near Bamber Bridge. Woodland, meadows, lakes, rivers and landscaped gardens all feature in this 650-acre (263 ha) park. There's also a visitor centre, walking and cycle trails and remnants of the area's industrial past. Tel 01772 324436 or visit www.cuerdenvalleypark.org.uk.

Gresgarth Hall, Caton. Leading landscape designer Arabella Lennox-Boyd has developed the gardens of her country home here over the last 30 years, reviving terraced, themed, vegetable and water gardens. Usually open for one Sunday a month in the summer. Visit www.arabellalennoxboyd.com/gresgarth.

Leighton Hall Garden, near Carnforth. The extensive parkland of the Gothic Leighton Hall features herb and walled gardens, herbaceous borders and trails through woodland. There are great views north to the Lake District.
Tel 01524 734474 or visit www.leightonhall.co.uk.

Myerscough College Gardens, Bilsbarrow. At what was once the Lancashire College of Agriculture, the varied gardens are still maintained by students. There's also a glasshouse of exotic plants and a tea room.
Tel 01995 642264 or visit www.myerscough.ac.uk.

Pendle Heritage Centre Garden, Barrowford. Neatly restored 18th-century walled garden, with an interesting little garden museum in an old potting shed.
Tel 01282 677152 or visit www.htnw.co.uk.

Rufford Old Hall Garden, near Ormskirk. The garden of this Tudor hall has been restored to its 19th-century state by the National Trust, and has lawns, topiary displays and garden trails.
Tel 01704 821254 or visit www.nationaltrust.org.uk.

Stanley Park, Blackpool. Several hundred acres of municipal parkland, landscaped for the town in the 1920s and featuring Italian, rose and remembrance gardens, water fountains and statues. There's room for a visitor centre, golf course, bowling greens, boating lake and cricket pitch too.
Tel 01253 478478 or visit www.friendsofstanleypark.org.uk.

Williamson Park, Lancaster. 50-acre (20 ha) city-centre park landscaped by James Williamson in the 1870s on a quarry from which much of the stone for Lancaster's buildings was mined. It features a large folly, the Ashton Memorial, added by Williamson's son.
Tel 01524 33318 or visit www.williamsonpark.com.

THE TWO THANKFUL VILLAGES

Of all the thousands of parishes across England from which men set out to fight in the First World War, only a handful could claim to be 'Thankful Villages' – places to which all the men from there returned afterwards. The list was first drawn up by Arthur Mee in his

King's England guide to the counties of England in the 1930s, though subsequent research has added a dozen more parishes.

Of these, Lancashire has just two: Arkholme and Nether Kellet. Between them, they shared around 80 men who left for the war and came home again, and remarkably they are located within 5 miles (8 km) of each other, near Carnforth in the far north of the county.

LANCASHIRE'S FOOTBALL MASCOTS

The mascots of each of the 15 football league clubs in Lancashire and, where there is one, the story of his, her or its connection with the side.

Accrington Stanley – **Winstanley**
Blackburn Rovers – **Roar the Lion**
Blackpool – **Bloomfield Bear**, named after the club's ground,
Bloomfield Road
Bolton Wanderers – **Lofty the Lion**, named after one of the
club's most famous former players, Nat Lofthouse
Burnley – **Bertie the Bee**
Bury – **Robbie the Bobbie**, named after Sir Robert Peel,
Prime Minister and founder of the Metropolitan Police Force
and born nearby
Everton – **Changy the Elephant**, named after the club's
sponsor, Chang; and **Mr Toffee**, inspired by the club's nickname,
the Toffees or Toffeemen. Toffee was once a speciality
of Everton
Liverpool – **Little Liver**, named after the mythical bird that is
the symbol of the city
Manchester City – **Moonchester**, named after Blue Moon,
a popular song among the club's fans
Manchester United – **Fred the Red**, a devil in honour of the
club's nickname, the Red Devils
Morecambe – **Christie the Cat**, named after the club's
old ground, Christie Park
Oldham Athletic – **Chaddy the Owl** in honour of the owl
on Oldham's town crest
Preston North End – **Deepdale Duck**, named after the
club's ground, Deepdale
Rochdale – **Desmond the Dragon**
Wigan Athletic – **Stripey the Laticat**, in honour of the club's
nickname, the Latics

LANCASHIRE FOOD –
CHORLEY AND ECCLES CAKES

There are strong rivalries over various foods in Lancashire – like cheese and black pudding to name just two – but the battle for supremacy between Chorley cakes and Eccles cakes is particularly fierce.

Both are small pastries stuffed with dried fruit – technically in fact not cakes at all – that are revered by the inhabitants of their respective towns and far and wide beyond. In Eccles, once a town in its own right but now part of Manchester's sprawl, the cakes are thought to have first been launched on a commercial basis in the late 18th century, when James Birch's shop on Vicarage Road started selling them. Recipes producing similar results date back even further, and there is evidence they were baked especially for religious festivals.

The reputation of Eccles cakes spread, first locally and then, as people of the town moved further afield, across the north. Sweet, buttery, filling and relatively cheap and easy to produce, they have endured while other local delicacies have disappeared. The leading manufacturer now is Lancashire Eccles Cakes, whose 70 staff turn out by hand more than half a million cakes a week for supermarkets and other outlets in the UK, as well as Lancashire ex-pats around the world. To many, the currant content means that Eccles cakes are known – with or without affection, depending on your taste – as 'dead fly pies' or 'squashed fly cakes'.

20 miles (32 km) northwest, the town of Chorley has probably been enjoying its own cakes for just as long as Eccles, and now celebrates its most famous food with an annual Chorley Cake Street Fair, originally staged to see who could bake the biggest. To the untrained eye the two varieties of cake might seem very similar, but woe betide anyone in either town who argues that there are no differences. While Eccles recipes generally use flaky puff pastry, Chorley ones use shortcrust, making for a flatter and more substantial cake. Eccles cakes are much the sweeter of the two, with sugar usually dusted on top, while Chorley's are more commonly eaten with a spread of butter, and perhaps some crumbly Lancashire cheese on the side.

Recipes for Eccles and Chorley cakes are closely guarded by their owners, each claiming a secret ingredient or technique that sets their finished cakes apart. Their popularity has also raised the question of whether any cakes baked commercially outside of the two towns can properly be called Eccles or Chorley cakes. Occasional moves have been made to have their production restricted – like champagne or parmesan – to their original homes, but so far they have come to little.

And there is nothing, of course, to stop Lancastrians and others savouring their own versions.

A recipe for Eccles cakes
500 g flaky puff pastry
200 g currants
100 g soft brown sugar
50 g mixed candied peel
25 g butter
Half a teaspoon of nutmeg and / or allspice, to taste
Plain flour
Milk or egg whites for glazing
Caster sugar for dusting

Gently melt the butter in a saucepan and stir in the sugar. Take it off the heat, and stir in the currants, candied peel and nutmeg or allspice. Dust a wo rking surface with flour, and roll out the pastry on top until it is about quarter of an inch (0.5 cm) thick. Cut it into rounds of about 4 inches (10 cm) across – you should get about twelve cakes with these quantities.

Now place a heaped teaspoonful of your fruit mixture into the centre of each round. Lightly brush half the circumference with water. Draw the edges of the pastry together over the fruit mixture and seal. Flip it over and pat down with your palm until it's flat again. Make a couple of slashes on the top of each. Brush lightly with milk or egg, and dust with caster sugar. Arrange on a greased baking tray, and bake in a hot oven (220°C / 425°F / gas mark 7) for about fifteen minutes, until slightly puffed up and browned at the edges. Cool on a wire rack.

For a rough approximation of this recipe for Chorley cakes, simply substitute the puff pastry for shortcrust and reduce the amount of sugar to a few tablespoons, with none scattered on top.

LANCASHIRE'S NATIONAL NATURE RESERVES

National Nature Reserves are areas of the country looked after by Natural England because of their special significance. They might have particularly rare or abundant wildlife, unusual and well preserved terrain or geology of particular interest, and all benefit from the extra care and protection that Reserve status confers. Just about all are at least partially open to the public, though it is worth checking restrictions before paying a special visit.

Of England's 222 National Nature Reserves Lancashire has 11, though several of these are to be found in the corners of the county now known, to the ire of many Lancastrians, as Cumbria and Merseyside. They are:

Ainsdale Sand Dunes. Extensive network of dunes on the coast between Liverpool and Southport, home to dozens of plant species as well as rare lizards, newts and toads.

Blelham Bog. Small 5-acre (2 ha) site of bogs and wet woodland, home to rare insects. More usually part of the Lake District, but just inside Lancashire's traditional borders.

Cabin Hill. Varied coastal terrain taking in sand flats, dunes, pasture and woodland and supporting a vast array of wildlife including natterjack toads.

Duddon Mosses. One of the best examples of raised mires in the country, home to marshy plants and birds including nightjar and curlew, at the head of the Duddon Estuary on Morecambe Bay.

Gait Barrows. Around 247 acres (100 ha) of limestone pavement plus associated bird and insect life and flora, close to the north end of Morecambe Bay.

North Fen. Small peatland reserve between Esthwaite Water and the Priest Pot near Hawkshead.

North Walney. Large slice of coastal terrain at the mouth of the Duddon Estuary, taking in dunes, slacks, salt marshes, heaths and grassland, and hosting rare birds and invertebrates.

Ribble Estuary. Several thousand acres of mud and sand flats and one of the biggest saltmarsh areas in the country, this is an important home for wintering waders and other birds.

Roudsea Wood and Mosses. Another richly varied reserve just off Morecambe Bay, taking in salt marshes, acid and limestone woodland and raised mires. Home to more than 500 plant and 250 fungi species.

Rusland Moss. 49 acres (20 ha) of unspoiled peatland in the Furness fells west of Windermere, surrounded by mosses and woodland.

Sandscale Haws. Lovely system of sand dunes, salt marshes, shingle and grassland on the Duddon Estuary, immediately adjacent to the North Walney reserve. An important sanctuary for natterjack toads in particular.

TWENTY FAMOUS PEOPLE WITH LANCASHIRE PLACES FOR NAMES

Rick ASTLEY	Nick HORNBY
Mike ATHERTON	Len HUTTON
Gordon BANKS	Burt LANCASTER
Tony BLACKBURN	Vivien LEIGH
Michael BOLTON	David MELLOR
Charlotte CHURCH	Eric MORECAMBE
Bing CROSBY	Horatio NELSON
John ENTWISTLE	Paula RADCLIFFE
Mick FLEETWOOD	Alexei SALE
George FORMBY	Kate THORNTON

DOES IT ALWAYS RAIN IN LANCASHIRE?

Despite what some visitors may think – no, it doesn't. But it is true that Lancashire gets a little more rain and a little less sunshine than most other parts of the UK.

As the 2008 figures below show, the northwest – a region defined by the Met Office as including Cumbria and Cheshire as well as Lancashire – gets around 50 per cent more rain than England's average. Just over half of the days of the year bring some rain in the northwest, compared to two days in five across England. And on average through the year, the northwest gets about 20 minutes less sunshine a day than England as a whole.

Lancashire also holds two of the UK's all-time rainfall records: for the most rain in five minutes – 1.25 inches (32 mm) in Preston in 1893 – and for the most in 90 minutes – 4.6 inches (117 mm) in Dunsop Bridge in 1967. Looking on the bright side, Lancashire would not be nearly so lush and green if it weren't for the rain. And while it is by some distance

the wettest region of England, it still gets about a tenth less rain and a
tenth more sunshine than Scotland.

	Northwest	England	UK
Mean temperature in °C (°F)	9.1 (48.4)	9.8 (49.6)	9.1 (48.4)
Hours of sunshine per day	3.8	4.1	3.6
Rainfall per week in inches (mm)	1.2 (29.5)	0.7 (18.5)	1 (25)
Days with rain in the year	184	145	169

GREAT LANCASTRIANS –
ERIC MORECAMBE

Not many Lancastrian entertainers have been so widely known and
enjoyed as Eric Morecambe – and even fewer have honoured the county
by naming themselves after their home towns.

John Eric Bartholomew was born in the seaside resort in 1926.
His mother encouraged his performing ambitions with singing, dancing
and music lessons, and it was at a talent contest in Hoylake on the Wirral
in 1939 that he first met Ernest Wiseman who, like Bartholomew, was
soon to adopt a new stage name. Both were inspired in their decision
by music hall star George Formby, whose family name was changed
from Booth after the town on the Lancashire coast.

Morecambe left school at 14 and began his double act with Wise in
comedy revues, but the pair's fledgling career was soon interrupted by
the Second World War. Towards the end of the war, Morecambe served
for a year as one of Britain's thousands of 'Bevin Boys' – young men who
worked in the coal mines, in his case at Accrington. Reunited by chance
after the war, Morecambe and Wise picked up their stage partnership
before graduating to radio and developing their own series on the
BBC's Northern Home Service. Their success prompted the BBC to offer
the pair a TV series in 1954, though the result, *Running Wild*, was a
disaster, slated by the critics and denting their confidence. They spent
the next few years working hard to improve their act, in revues, variety
performances and summer shows at Lancashire resorts like Blackpool
and Morecambe.

Their rehabilitation was complete when they won a series with ITV
in 1961. *Two of a Kind* struggled at first, but its blend of sketches,
catchphrases and recurring jokes and the on-screen chemistry of the
pair – Wise generally the straight man to Morecambe's daft comic –
soon struck a chord with the public, many of whom were discovering
television for the first time. Morecambe, a heavy smoker and drinker

and his health possibly damaged by his year in the coal mines, suffered a heart attack in 1968, but after several months of rest returned to TV. By now on the BBC, the double act developed with the help of new scriptwriters and frequent celebrity guests, and ratings continued to soar, especially for their annual Christmas shows. At their peak, in 1977, the Christmas Day edition drew 28 million viewers – half the population at the time. No British entertainment broadcast before or since has come close to that figure.

Morecambe and Wise switched back to ITV the next year, and while the show remained popular, the double act started to lose some of its spark. The stress of performing had contributed to Morecambe's second heart attack in 1979, and he died after a third in 1984, shortly after coming off stage in Gloucestershire. Tributes to him – and to Wise, who died in 1999, also from a heart attack – were numerous and sincere, and the pair's performances remain hugely popular and influential to other comedians.

The town of Morecambe paid tribute to its most famous son with a statue of him on the promenade in classic comic pose, unveiled by the Queen in 1999 and inscribed with some of his catchphrases and the names of 103 celebrities he performed with. There is also a plaque on the house where he was born on Buxton Street in the town. Not far away at the Leighton Moss reserve near Carnforth, a bird hide and pool are both named in honour of Morecambe, a keen birdwatcher.

LANCASHIRE ON SCREEN – CORONATION STREET

Firmly rooted in the red rose county and one of Britain's most successful TV shows over five decades, *Coronation Street* is a Lancashire institution.

When the show's creator, Tony Warren, devised his fictional town of Weatherfield, he based it and its characters on both his hometown of Swinton and nearby Salford, where the programme was filmed. These days the show is largely shot at studios in central Manchester, but the street's cobbled roads, rows of terraced houses, gossipy corner shop and no-nonsense pub all mean Weatherfield has more in common with small-town or suburban life than with prosperous city centres. Either way, it's unmistakeably Lancastrian.

Warren's *Coronation Street* first aired on 9 December 1960, and at first only 12 episodes were commissioned for the Granada region. The response from the mostly southern-based critics was mixed, one concluding that 'The programme is doomed from the outset with its dreary signature tune and grim scene of terraced houses and smoking chimneys.'Viewers, though, and those in the north in particular, quickly warmed to its characters, and by 1964 the show was regularly drawing 15 to 20 million viewers.

Its popularity has fluctuated over the years as actors come and go, and viewing numbers are now nearer 10 million, but its blend of distinctive characters, dramatic storylines and northern humour means its future has never been seriously threatened. *Coronation Street* has notched up more than 7,000 episodes since that début in 1960, making it the longest running soap on British TV, and despite the decline in terrestrial TV viewing and advertising, its appeal is still strong. The show is exported around the world too, and is a nostalgic taste of home for many Lancashire ex-pats far from home.

It is a mark of *Coronation Street's* popularity and realism that Manchester taxi drivers are often asked to take new arrivals in the city to Weatherfield. Although they have never been able to oblige, they did in the past direct devotees to Granada's set, where they could walk the show's cobbled streets or drink in the Rover's Return. Those tours ended in 2000, though they may return as the show enters its second half-century.

LANCASHIRE'S CRICKET RECORDS

Lancashire County Cricket Club has a long and proud history dating back to its formation in 1864. Here are some of the club's most important team, batting, bowling and fielding records since then, drawn from all first-class cricket up to the start of the 2010 season.

863 . . . . highest team score, v Surrey in 1990
707 for 9 . . . . highest opposition score, by Surrey in 1990
25 . . . . lowest team score, v Derbyshire in 1871
22 . . . . lowest opposition score, by Glamorgan in 1924
1,650 . . . . most runs in a single match, v Surrey in 1990
221 . . . . fewest runs in a single match, v Surrey in 1888
Innings and 445 runs . . . . . . largest margin of victory, v Hampshire in 1911
Innings and 220 runs . . . . . . largest margin of defeat, v West Indies in 1950
1 run . . . . narrowest margin of victory, v Leicestershire in 1906 and v Hampshire in 1920; and narrowest margin of defeat, v Surrey in 1948

424 . . . highest innings score, by Archie MacLaren, v Somerset in 1895

315 not out . . . . highest innings score against, by Thomas Hayward for Surrey in 1898

2,633 . . . . most runs in a season, by Johnny Tyldesley in 1901

11 . . . . most centuries in a season, by Charles Hallows in 1928

13 . . . . most ducks in a season, by Keith Goodwin in 1965

34,222 . . . . most career runs, by Ernest Tyldesley, 1909-36

90 . . . . most career centuries, by Ernest Tyldesley, 1909-36

89 . . . . most career ducks, by Brian Statham, 1950-68

371 . . . . highest partnership for any wicket, by Frank Watson and Ernest Tyldesely for the second wicket, v Surrey in 1928

10 for 46 . . . . best innings bowling figures, by William Hickton v Hampshire in 1870

17 for 91 . . . . best match bowling figures, by Harry Dean v Yorkshire in 1913

10 for 40 . . . best innings bowling figures against, by Gubby Allen for Middlesex in 1929

16 for 65 . . . . . best match bowling figures against, by George Giffen for the Australians in 1886

198 . . . . most wickets in a season, by Ted McDonald in 1925

1,816 . . . . most career wickets, by Brian Statham, 1950-68

7 . . . . most wicket-keeping victims in an innings, by Bill Farrimond v Kent in 1930, Warren Hegg v Derbyshire in 1989 and Luke Sutton v Yorkshire in 2008

11 . . . . most wicket-keeping victims in a match, by Warren Hegg v Derbyshire in 1989

97 . . . . most wicket-keeping victims in a season, by George Duckworth in 1928

925 . . . . most wicket-keeping victims in a career, by George Duckworth, 1923-47

6 . . . . most outfield catches in an innings, by Ken Grieves v Sussex in 1951

8 . . . . most outfield catches in a match, by Ken Grieves v Sussex in 1951

63 . . . . most outfield catches in a season, by Ken Grieves in 1950

555 . . . . most outfield catches in a Lancashire career, by Ken Grieves, 1945-64

573 . . . . . most first-class matches for Lancashire, by Ernest Tyldesley, 1909-36

MUSICIANS FROM LANCASHIRE

With its twin capitals of Manchester and Liverpool, Lancashire's music scene has long been the richest of any region of the country, with the possible exception of London. Here are 40 of the county's best known singers, songwriters, bands and composers, together with their places of birth or formation.

10cc (Manchester)
Rick Astley (Newton-le-Willows)
Badly Drawn Boy (Bolton)
The Beatles (Liverpool)
Harrington Birtwistle (Accrington)
Elkie Brooks (Salford)
The Buzzcocks (Manchester)
The Charlatans (Manchester)
Elvis Costello (Liverpool)
Peter Maxwell Davies (Salford)
Doves (Manchester)
Elbow (Bury)
The Fall (Manchester)
Kathleen Ferrier (Higher Walton)
Gracie Fields (Rochdale)
Wayne Fontana (Manchester)
George Formby (Wigan)
Billy Fury (Liverpool)
Freddie Garrity (Manchester)
David Gray (Manchester)

The Happy Mondays (Salford)
Roy Harper (Manchester)
Herman's Hermits (Manchester)
The Hollies (Manchester)
John Ireland (Manchester)
Davy Jones (Manchester)
Joy Division (Manchester)
Graham Nash (Blackpool)
Oasis (Manchester)
Mark Owen (Oldham)
Simply Red (Manchester)
The Smiths (Manchester)
Lisa Stansfield (Heywood)
Ronald Stevenson (Blackburn)
The Stone Roses (Manchester)
Eva Turner (Oldham)
Frankie Vaughan (Liverpool)
The Verve (Wigan)
William Walton (Oldham)
Russell Watson (Salford)

SOME UNUSUAL PUB NAMES

Lancashire's hundreds of pubs include plenty of common names: Red Lions, Royal Oaks, White Harts, Crowns and so on. But it also has a handful with some weird and wonderful names, many of them dating back a century or more. Here are 15 of the most unusual.

Hark to Dandler, Bury

Help Me Through Inn, Bury

Peveril of the Peak, Manchester

Same Yet, Prestwich

The Ape and Apple, Manchester

The Clog and Billycock, Pleasington

The Duck and Puddle, Blackburn

The Fly in the Loaf, Liverpool

The Hand and Dagger, Kirkham

The Happy Man, Wythenshawe

The Pig on the Wall, Droylesden

The Smut Inn, Oldham

The Spanking Roger, Manchester

The Swan with Two Necks, Pendleton

The Weighing Machine, Liverpool

The town of Stalybridge on the Lancashire-Cheshire border meanwhile boasts the pubs with both the longest and the shortest names in the UK: the Old Thirteenth Cheshire Astley Volunteer Rifleman Corps Inn on Astley Street, understandably better known locally as the Rifleman; and Q, half a mile away on Market Street.

J R R TOLKIEN AND LANCASHIRE

Was Lancashire the inspiration for *The Lord of the Rings*? It might be stretching things a little to say that, but J R R Tolkien's associations with the county are certainly strong.

They began during the Second World War when Tolkien's son, John, moved to St Mary's Hall at Stonyhurst College in the Ribble Valley near Clitheroe to study for the priesthood, having been evacuated from his seminary in Rome. As frequent entries in the college's visitors' book prove, Tolkien often came to stay nearby, and he was soon captivated by the wooded countryside and brooding hills around Stonyhurst and in the Forest of Bowland.

Throughout the 1940s, Tolkien was composing his epic *The Lord of the Rings* trilogy, and aspects of the Lancashire countryside can be detected in the books' Middle Earth landscape. Some of the area's place names are very similar to those Tolkien created - like the book's River

Shirebourn, inspired by the Ribble and named after the Shireburn family who built Stonyhurst. Tolkien may well also have been intrigued by nearby Pendle Hill and its association with witches, sorcery and mysterious goings-on in the 17th century, and a likeness can be detected in the books' mountain ranges.

Other claimed links, like Hurst Green being the inspiration for Frodo Baggins' home of Hobbiton, may be more tenuous. But Tolkien is certainly known to have written parts of *The Lord of the Rings* in Lancashire, working in both a classroom at Stonyhurst and the guest-house in its grounds where he stayed. And he continued his association with Stonyhurst after John had moved on, since another of his sons taught there in the 1970s, and he came back often. St Mary's Hall, now a preparatory school for the Catholic Stonyhurst College, has named its Tolkien Library in the author's honour.

Since a trilogy of film adaptations caused interest in Tolkien to surge, Ribble Valley's council has tried to capitalise on its associations by creating a 5-mile (8 km) Tolkien Trail, starting and finishing at Hurst Green. St Mary's Hall and Stonyhurst are also both open to the public during the summer holidays.

Stonyhurst boasts a second major literary association – with Arthur Conan Doyle, a student there in the 1860s. The college is thought to have inspired some of the scenes in his books, especially *The Hound of the Baskervilles*, and its records show that boys named Sherlock and Moriarty – Holmes' arch-enemy – were contemporaries of Doyle.

THE CLOCK THAT STRIKES 13

The town of Worsley near Salford was, after the construction of the Bridgewater Canal, an important centre for industrialising Lancashire. It is now a conservation area and part of a proposed World Heritage site, with a handful of reminders of its significance to industries like coal, iron and cotton. Less well known is that it is also home to a perhaps the only clock in the world that once a day strikes 13 instead of one. When asked why they were consistently late returning from their lunch break at 1 p.m., workers for the Duke of Bridgewater protested that they had not heard the clock strike one – so the Duke promptly had the mechanism changed to produce 13 peals instead. The clock has since been moved to the town's church, but it continues its unusual ringing.

1974 AND LANCASHIRE OLD AND NEW

What, exactly, is Lancashire? Until 1974, the answer was pretty clear. The ancient red rose county had been established since the 12th century and had endured invasions and social upheaval. It stretched as far north as the Lake District villages of Coniston and Hawkshead, as far south as Liverpool and Warrington, and as far east as Manchester and Oldham.

But in the early 1970s, the government drew up plans to redefine the boundaries of local councils, changing the borders of Britain's 86 historic counties at a few strokes of a civil servant's pen. Out went ancient county names with which local people had identified for centuries, like the three Ridings of Yorkshire, Westmorland and Cumberland, and in came entirely new entities in a tiered system of local government. The act was passed on 1 April 1974, the irony of the date not passing unnoticed.

In Lancashire, the northernmost tranche of the historic county was sliced off overnight and transferred to Cumbria. Liverpool and much of the area around it was chipped off to become Merseyside, and Manchester and its satellite towns became Greater Manchester. A small area of southern Lancashire went to Cheshire, while in the northeast of the county it actually expanded, by drawing in a piece of the old West Riding of Yorkshire. The end result was a vastly reduced Lancashire – its area slashed by nearly half and its population plummeting from around 5 million people at its peak to just over 1 million now – and a new jumble of counties on the map of the northwest.

At the time the changes were made, the government insisted that they were purely for administrative purposes, and that the ancient county borders remained intact. That didn't ease the understandable confusion, however, and ever since 1974 the public and the media have gradually identified more closely with the new counties. Many of those living in Furness, for instance, would now call Cumbria home, despite their area having been part of Lancashire for centuries and retaining a Lancashire postcode. Liverpudlians, meanwhile, are under the umbrellas of both their city's council and the Merseyside metropolitan county, inevitably diluting their allegiance to Lancashire. Subsequent tinkering to local government boundaries, especially in Merseyside and Greater Manchester, has only added to the uncertainty.

The changes infuriated loyal Lancastrians when they were introduced, and many have studiously ignored them ever since. Lancashire is still widely used for identification in the 'lost' parts of the county – on people's addresses, for instance, and by clubs and societies. The Friends of Real Lancashire campaigns for the old boundaries to be preserved for ceremonial and cultural purposes, and promotes in particular the association of cities like Liverpool and Manchester with the county rather than with Merseyside and Greater Manchester. Other activists like County Watch have gone further, removing 'Welcome to Lancashire' road signs from locations they consider wrong and replanting them on the county's ancient borders.

FAMOUS LANCASHIRE BUSINESSES

As well as the famous Lancashire-born companies profiled elsewhere in this book, like Tate & Lyle, the Co-op and Unilever, the county has produced dozens more successful businesses. Here are ten of the best known exports.

Beechams. Thomas Beecham started his pharmaceutical business with a shop in Wigan in 1847, before opening a factory in St Helens 12 years later. Beechams is now part of the GlaxoSmithKline empire, but the name lives on in some products.

Booths. Little known outside of the northwest, Booths is a chain of supermarkets that was started by Bury-born Edwin Booth in 1847 with a modest shop in Blackpool. Despite rumours of approaches from other supermarkets, the business remains in the Booth family.

The Guardian. The newspaper was founded in Manchester in 1821 by the noted Lancashire-based reformer John Edward Taylor, and was known as the Manchester Guardian until 1959. It retains offices in Manchester today.

H Samuel. The modern jewellery business grew out of a Manchester shop opened by Harriet (H) Samuel, part of the well-known clock and watch making family in the 18th and 19th centuries. It remained a family business until 1986.

Pilkington. Created in St Helens in the 1820s by the Pilkington family, the glass maker employed some 10,000 people at its peak. It continues to be based in the town, though it now has Japanese owners.

Shearings. The coach company was founded by Herbert Shearing after he moved to Oldham in the 1920s. The firm has changed hands plenty of times since but the Shearings name has endured and its headquarters are now in Wigan.

Timpsons. This chain of several hundred repair, key cutting and dry cleaning shops was founded by William Timpson in Manchester in 1865 and is now run by his great-grandson.

Uncle Joe's Mint Balls. This hugely popular Lancashire sweet was first made by William and Ellen Santus in Wigan in the late 1890s, and is still manufactured in the town in much the same way. Uncle Joe was probably a fictional character.

Vimto. The purple concoction of fruit juices, herbs and flavourings was created by Noel Nichols in Manchester in 1908, and was soon popular in herbalist shops and temperance bars in particular. There is a statue of a bottle of Vimto on the spot in Manchester where it was first made.

Warburtons. The bread-making business grew out of a grocer's shop opened in Bolton by Thomas and George Warburton in the 1870s, and was developed by George's son Henry. The business continues to be run by the Warburton family from Lancashire, and still owns the site of the first shop in Bolton.

ᘓᘒᘓᘒᘓᘒᘓᘒᘓᘒᘓᘒᘓᘒᘓᘒᘓᘒᘓᘒᘓᘒ

LANCASHIRE'S PLACE IN THE WORLD

Lancashire's population of around 1.1 million people means it has a larger population than Fiji but a smaller one than Swaziland. As this table shows, if Lancashire were a country it would rank in the same league as some far-flung and glamorous states. The figure of 1.1 million is the total for the modern administrative county, and there fo re excludes large areas that are part of ceremonial Lancashire but are now classified elsewhere. Population estimates for countries are from *The CIA World Factbook* for 2009.

Country	Population
Trinidad and Tobago	1,229,953
Timor-Leste	1,131,612
Swaziland	1,123,913
Lancashire	**1,134,976**
Fiji	944,720
Qatar	833,285
Cyprus	796,740

Area-wise, Lancashire is larger than Samoa and Luxemburg and smaller than the remote British territory of South Georgia and the South Sandwich Islands in the Atlantic.

Country	Area in sq miles (sq km)
French Polynesia	1,609 (4,167)
Cape Verde	1,557 (4,033)
South Georgia and the South Sandwich Islands	1,507 (3,903)
Lancashire	**1,121 (2,903)**
Samoa	1,093 (2,831)
Luxemburg	998 (2,586)
Comoros	477 (1,235)

THE LANCASHIRE MONOPOLY BOARD

Bamber Bridge near Preston has the cheapest property in Lancashire, while Lancaster Castle is the most expensive place to rent. That, at least, is the verdict of the Lancashire Monopoly board in a special localised version of the classic family game.

The edition replaces each of the famous original London properties from Old Kent Road to Mayfair with various Lancashire locations. They take in some well-known streets in Bolton, Preston and Blackburn among other towns and cities, plus several football grounds and tourist spots like Blackpool's Pleasure Beach and Tower. The game caused something of a fuss when it was released, with people living in streets or towns that were placed in the lower price brackets regarding it as something of an insult. In ascending order of value, Lancashire's 22 Monopoly properties are:

Bamber Bridge
Great Eccleston
Ribble Valley
Blackpool Pleasure Beach
Deepdale Stadium, Preston
Elwood Park, Blackburn
Reebok Stadium, Bolton
JJB Stadium, Wigan
St James Street, Burnley
Avroe Crescent, Blackpool
Whalley

Mallison Street, Bolton
Fleetwood
Baxenden
Bromley Cross, Bolton
Gracie Fields Theatre, Rochdale
Market Square, Preston
Lord Street, Southport
South King Street, Blackpool
Richmond Terrace, Blackburn
Blackpool Tower and Circus
Lancaster Castle

The four station properties on the board are Blackpool Airport, Bolton Street Station in Bury, Lancaster Canal and Leyland.

LANCASHIRE FOOD – CHEESE

Lancashire's cheese is among the best in Britain and one of the county's most popular food exports. Its producers claim the cheese tradition dates back as far as the 13th century, and it has certainly been manufactured for as long as farms have kept cows and had excess milk to use up. But it wasn't until the late 19th century that Lancashire's cheese began to develop the taste and reputation that we know today, thanks to concerted efforts among producers to standardise its method of production. That method involves blending curds from successive days' milking, and it is still the way much of Lancashire's cheese gets its distinctive taste.

The cheese is commonly broken down into three styles: crumbly, which is only briefly matured for a mild, milky taste; creamy, aged for longer for a richer, buttery flavour; and tasty, an even more mature version of creamy and a strong, nutty cheese. Crumbly is the most recently developed style and the easiest to produce, since it is made from one rather than multiple milkings. It is this that supermarkets and other large retailers commonly sell, having appropriated the Lancashire name for a cheese that is quickly and cheaply manufactured in vast quantities. The real deal, though, hand made by dedicated specialists and matured for months rather than weeks – and, in the case of tasty Lancashire, for as long as two years – is a far superior cheese, complex and quite unique in flavour.

While once there were hundreds of small farms turning out cheese, now there are perhaps a dozen significant producers. Many of them, though, are now doing very well, and are co-operating on efforts to market Lancashire cheese as a distinctive brand. Some of the best producers are based in and around the Forest of Bowland, often collecting milk from nearby farms and using recipes passed down through several generations.

Lancashire's cheese is great in everyday sandwiches or on toast, but it is also a popular and versatile ingredient in cooking, perhaps crumbled into pasta, risottos or omelettes, integrated into a pie's filling or topping, or scattered into salads. For the ultimate Lancashire snack, enjoy a slice of the cheese with a buttered Chorley cake and a mug of strong tea.

THE LOST RAILWAYS

What do Bacup, Standish, Wrea Green and Great Harwood all have in common? Fleetwood, Knott End-on-Sea, Longridge and Cherry Tree? Among many others, they are all places that were once home to stations on Lancashire's thriving railway network, and shut in the rationalisation of Britain's railways that took place in the couple of decades after the Second World War. Here are ten of the many branches that once made up a cobweb of lines around Lancashire but which are now lost.

Bolton to Kenyon Junction
George Stephenson was the chief engineer on this 9-mile (14 km) line, put up to link Bolton with the coalfields to the south. It took passengers for a while too, but was abandoned in the 1960s.

Bury to Bacup
Opened in 1846 to run from Bury to Bacup via Ramsbottom and Rawtenstall. Closed in the 1970s but soon revived by the steam enthusiasts of the East Lancashire Railway and now a thriving heritage line.

Chorley to Cherry Tree
A joint venture between two big railway companies to link Lancashire's coal and textile centres, the line's engineers had to cross canals and negotiate challenging gradients. It was decommissioned in 1968.

Garstang to Knott End
12 miles (19 km) of line running from the Garstang intersection with the Lancaster and Preston Railway to the Wyre Estuary opposite Fleetwood at Knott End-on-Sea. Its owners always struggled to make it pay, and it closed to passengers in 1930, though goods trains occasionally used it until 1965. Some of the route survives as a footpath.

Great Harwood to Rose Grove
A 9-mile (14 km) loop that connected industrial towns to the Lancashire and Yorkshire Railway, it also helped ferry workers to the coast during the summer. Passenger trains were withdrawn in 1957 and freight ones seven years later.

Lowton St Mary's to St Helens

This 8-mile (13 km) line was in financial trouble from the start,
opening several years late in 1895. It took colliery and goods
traffic and occasionally ferried race-goers to its Haydock Park stop,
but it was wound down in the 1950s.

Oldham to Guide Bridge

A branch line linking Ashton-under-Lyne with major railways
at Oldham. It was yet another to succumb to competition from
road transport and rail rationalisation in the 1960s.

Ormskirk to St Helens

This 12-mile (19 km) line was built largely to link the growing
number of coal towns, but it struggled for passengers and
was closed to them in the 1950s, soon after the railways
were nationalised.

Preston to Fleetwood

Sir Peter Hesketh Fleetwood funded the rail link to the town
that bears his name in 1840, and it was particularly popular for
its onward ferry links to Ireland and the Isle of Man. Passenger
numbers fell when ferry routes switched, and the line was
mothballed in the 1960s, though there is now a campaign to
restore trains to Fleetwood.

Preston to Longridge

Opened in 1839 to carry stone from the Ribble Valley quarries
to Preston and on to Liverpool. At its peak there were plans to
link the line into Yorkshire, but declining use led to passenger and
freight services being pulled in the 1930s and 1960s respectively.

꧁꧂꧁꧂꧁꧂꧁꧂꧁꧂꧁꧂꧁꧂꧁꧂꧁꧂꧁꧂꧁꧂꧁꧂꧁꧂

GREAT LANCASTRIANS –
EMMELINE PANKHURST

Few Lancashire-born people have had as profound an effect on British
social and political history as Emmeline Pankhurst and her daughters.
And aside from The Beatles, Emmeline is the only Lancastrian on the
Time 100, the famous US magazine's list of the 100 most important
people of the 20th century.

Emmeline Goulden was born in 1858 in the Moss Side suburb of
Manchester, into a family with a tradition of radical politics. At 21 she

married Richard Pankhurst, a reformist lawyer and ardent supporter of the women's suffrage movement, and in 1889 she became involved in the Women's Franchise League, which campaigned, successfully, to get married women the vote in local elections. Increasingly frustrated by the indifference with which public speaking and peaceful protest were met, in 1903 she founded the more militant Women's Social and Political Union, which soon became infamous for its passionate protests and no little trouble making. Partly inspired by Emmeline's reverence for the French Revolution, marches, window smashing, arson and hunger strikes all became part of the tactics. Most famously of all, in 1913 union member Emily Davison was killed when she threw herself in front of the King's horse at the Derby.

Having sold her Manchester home and moved to London in 1907, Emmeline started traveling more widely to build support for the movement, across the US as well as the UK. Frequently arrested, she was among the many hunger strikers who were brutally force fed, and jailed on a dozen separate occasions in 1912 alone as authorities played a cat and mouse game, releasing strikers from prison only to return them there when they had regained their strength.

Pankhurst was joined in her causes by her daughters, also born in Manchester. Their talents were complementary and formidable – the first, Christabel, a committed and often forceful agitator, and the second, Sylvia, a more contemplative socialist who also fought against other injustices. But disagreements over policy led to some painful splits in the family in later years, not least during the First World War, when Emmeline and Christabel suspended the suffrage campaign to support the country's effort while Sylvia, a pacifist, protested against it. A third daughter, Adela, emigrated to Australia just before the war and never saw her mother again.

The vote was finally granted to women over 30, with limitations, at the end of the war in 1918. Emmeline died in 1928, just a few weeks after women's voting rights were brought fully into line with men's. Some historians think the increasingly aggressive tactics adopted by Emmeline and her supporters did their cause more harm than good, but the Pankhursts are more usually given much of the credit for winning women the vote, along with other rights before and since like equality in pay and divorce and inheritance settlements. They also paved the way for far greater female involvement in British politics.

Decades on it is hard to imagine that women had to fight so hard for such basic rights, but the Pankhursts were well ahead of their own era, and their vocal, violent protests stunned and ruptured Edwardian Britain. 'She shaped an idea of women for our time,' said *Time* magazine in its citation of Emmeline. 'She shook society into a new pattern from which there could be no going back.'

The Manchester home of Emmeline, Christabel, Sylvia and Adela is now the Pankhurst Centre, containing a small museum and a recreation of the rooms where they planned suffrage campaigns. Opening hours are limited; tel 0161 273 5673 for details. There is also a statue of Emmeline in London's Victoria Tower Gardens, close to Parliament in Westminster.

BIRDWATCHING IN LANCASHIRE

Lancashire's most common bird is the starling, according to the annual Big Garden Birdwatch survey by the Royal Society for the Protection of Birds. The top ten birds in the county, together with the average number of times they were spotted in a garden by participants on a single day in the 2009 survey, are:

1	Starling	4.77
2	House sparrow	3.50
3	Blackbird	2.77
4	Blue tit	2.25
5	Collared dove	1.60
6	Chaffinch	1.57
7	Long tailed tit	1.41
8	Goldfinch	1.30
9	Great tit	1.26
10	Robin	1.25

LEAGUE V UNION:
LANCASHIRE AND RUGBY

It was a Lancastrian – Salford-born William Webb Ellis – who, according to folklore, began the sport of rugby when he picked up the ball and ran with it during a game of football. And here, two centuries on and in one code of the game at least, rugby is as popular and passionately supported as anywhere.

Although the sport's governing bodies and many of its leading clubs were based in London, Lancashire soon became one of rugby's heartlands. Its reputation for skilful players and successful clubs grew with the rise of its industry, the mills and mines producing a steady flow of talented and strong sportsmen. But as the sport became more organised, the difficulties of balancing it with work, and of playing a hard game of rugby after long hours in the pits or factories, became apparent. Some clubs started to compensate their leading players for their appearances, paying 'broken time' money to make up for the work hours they had sacrificed to train and play, and increasing sums were offered to lure stars away from rival clubs.

Payments were made covertly at first, but as they became more common, north-south and class divides began to open up. Rugby's southern clubs largely played for pleasure and pride, and they and the game's rulers were dismayed at the thinly veiled and unseemly professionalism in working class Lancashire and Yorkshire. In the early 1890s several northern clubs were punished with suspensions for making 'illegal' payments, cranking up the tension and resentment. Then, in 1895, came rugby's great schism, when 22 clubs resigned from England's Rugby Football Union to form a new northern union among themselves. The famous meeting was held in Huddersfield and then, as now, slightly more clubs hailed from Yorkshire, but the 22 founding members included nine from Lancashire: Broughton, Leigh, Oldham, Rochdale, St Helens, Tyldesley, Warrington, Widnes and Wigan. Dozens more followed over the next few years.

For a while, the two rival unions played rugby under the same rules, but after a similar breakaway in Australia a distinctive code began to emerge. Sides were reduced from 15 to 13 players, a new scoring system was introduced, and by 1922, when the Northern Union became known as the Rugby Football League, the sport was much changed from the old rugby.

Although both forms of rugby have since spread, around the world as well as Britain, Lancashire and Yorkshire remain the main enclaves of league. Lancashire clubs like Wigan, St Helens and Warrington are prominent in the top tier of rugby league most years, while in the equivalent division in union, only Sale tends to rival for honours. Mostly amiable hostilities continue in the sport in the north - between league and union over which is the better sport; between Lancashire and Yorkshire over which is the strongest county; and between counties' own clubs, for all-important local bragging rights.

TEN UNUSUAL MUSEUMS

Lancashire has dozens of excellent museums, and can boast that among them are some of the country's - if not the world's - leading authorities on commercial vehicles, fire fighting, hats and lawnmowers. Often the result of someone's personal passion and staffed by volunteers, these places might seem somewhat limited in their appeal, but they are worth a visit. Here are ten of Lancashire's quirkiest museums.

The Beatles Story, Liverpool.
Hugely popular exhibition of Liverpool's most famous musical sons. The childhood homes of Paul McCartney and John Lennon are also both opened to the public by the National Trust.
Tel 0151 709 1963 or visit www.beatlesstory.com.

The British Commercial Vehicle Museum, Leyland.
Everything you ever wanted to know about trucks and buses through the years, in a town that owes much of its history to the commercial vehicle industry.
Tel 01772 451011 or visit www.bcvm.org.uk.

The British in India Museum, Nelson.
The story of colonial rule, with exhibits including tiger skins and the last Union Jack lowered in Lucknow, all somewhat incongruously located in the old mill town of Nelson.
Tel 01282 613129 or visit www.britishinindiamuseum.co.uk.

British Lawnmower Museum, Southport.
Heaven for mower fans, who will find examples of machines through the ages and some lawnmowers of the rich and famous. Museum motto: 'It's mower interesting'.
Tel 01704 501336 or visit www.lawnmowerworld.com.

Greater Manchester Fire Service Museum, Manchester.
Exhibits showing fire fighting through the ages, lovingly looked after by the museum's volunteers.
Tel 01706 901227 or visit www.manchesterfire.gov.uk.

Laurel and Hardy Museum, Ulverston.
Stan Laurel was born in Ulverston, and this museum grew out of one man's affection for the comic duo.
Tel 01229 582292 or visit www.laurel-and-hardy-museum.co.uk.

Museum of Lancashire, Preston.
The best place to find out more about the heritage of the red rose county.
Tel 01772 534075 or visit www.lancashire.gov.uk.

National Football Museum.
Excellent museum dedicated to English football,
initially housed in Preston but relocating to Manchester in 2011.
Visit www.nationalfootballmuseum.com.

North West Museum of Road Transport, St Helens.
Great if you love old buses and cars; not so much fun if you don't.
Tel 01744 451681 or visit www.hallstreetdepot.info.

Queen Street Mill Textile Museum, Burnley.
The world's only surviving 19th-century steam powered weaving
mill, in a town that was once dominated by the textile industry.
Tel 01282 412555 or visit www.lancashire.gov.uk.

MOUNTAIN RESCUE IN NUMBERS

Some figures from the 2008 report of the Rossendale and Pendle
Mountain Rescue Team, which looks after a 350-square mile (906 sq km)
portion of Lancashire from just south of Bury to just north of Clitheroe.

45 . . . . incidents attended

1,672 . . . . hours spent by members attending incidents

37 . . . . average man-hours spent per incident

10.4 . . . . . average number of team members attending each incident

47 . . . . members of the public involved in incidents

6 . . . . number of children involved in incidents

0 . . . . number of animals involved in accidents

12 . . . . incidents occurring on Saturdays,
the most common day for call-outs

2 . . . . incidents occurring on Wednesdays,
the least common day for call-outs

23 . . . . incidents occurring between 12 p.m. and 6 p.m.,
the most common time for call-outs

5 . . . . fatalities in incidents

LANCASHIRE SAYINGS

Lancashire has hundreds of dialect phrases and sayings. Here are ten of the most expressive.

Ah cud eyt a buttered frog	I'm very hungry
Ahm spittin' feathers	I'm very thirsty
Ah were up at sparrow's fart	I had to rise very early
Ee's fair bowlegged wi' brass	He's very rich
Ah were standin' theer leyke cheese at fourpence	I was hanging around with nothing to do
Tha's no oil in thi lamp	You are a fool
Tha meks a betta dooar than a winda	You are blocking my view
Tha's a face like a line a wet weshin'	You are looking rather miserable
Pigs waint follow an empty bucket	People won't work for nothing
Put wood i' th' oil!	Close the door!

LANCASHIRE'S BEST PICNIC SPOT

Lancashire's tourist board promotes picnics as a good way to enjoy the county's countryside, and in 2008 surveyed visitors about their favourite spots. The winner, favoured by almost a third of people, was the Trough of Bowland, the valley dividing the Forest of Bowland and an officially designated Area of Outstanding Natural Beauty. Close behind in second was Morecambe Bay, the vast expanse of sand that forms a large chunk of Lancashire's coast.

Visit Lancashire's same survey also uncovered the food most commonly associated with the red rose county: Lancashire Hot Pot. The most popular drink, meanwhile, was Lancashire tea, followed by two beers – Lancaster Bomber and Pendle Witches Brew – and sarsaparilla, the herbal soft drink made popular in Lancashire by the temperance movement.

LANCASHIRE GRACE

An appropriately no-nonsense and irreverent version of the traditional blessing, recited by Lancastrians at the table before their main meal of the day.

> 'Bless o' on us Lord wi' this gradely stuff,
> An' nudge me when ah've 'ad enogh.'

NATIONAL TRUST PROPERTIES IN LANCASHIRE

The National Trust looks after ten properties in Lancashire, including four in the northernmost part of the county in the southern Lake District and four in Liverpool. The properties are:

Beatrix Potter Gallery, Hawkshead. Potter's sketches and watercolours are on display in this pretty 17th-century cottage, once the office of Potter's solicitor husband.

Cartmel Priory Gatehouse, Cartmel. A 14th-century fortified gatehouse to Cartmel's famous priory with rooms inside occasionally opened to the public.

Dalton Castle, Dalton-in-Furness. A 14th-century tower, built by the Abbot of nearby Furness Abbey. There's an exhibition of local history inside.

20 Forthlin Road, Allerton. The Liverpool childhood home of Paul McCartney is where The Beatles rehearsed in their early days.

Gawthorpe Hall, Padiham. In the hub of industrial Lancashire, this Elizabethan house is an oasis of calm, with fine gardens and rooms packed with portraits and textile collections.

Mr Hardman's Photographic Studio, Liverpool. The Georgian terraced house of Edward Chambré Hardman, a renowned photographer of Liverpool people and places, and preserved as it was in his time.

Hill Top, Near Sawrey. The 17th-century farmhouse of Beatrix Potter. She wrote many of her books here, inspired by the surrounding countryside.

Mendips, Woolton. The home in the Liverpool suburbs of John Lennon and his Aunt Mimi – like McCartney's house an important stop on any Beatles pilgrimage to the city.

Rufford Old Hall, Rufford. Tudor house with fine furniture and tapestry collections. William Shakespeare is thought to have stayed and performed here when he was young.

Speke Hall, Liverpool. Magnificent large Tudor house with a well preserved great hall, kitchen and servants' quarters, plus good walks in the wooded grounds.

In addition to these properties, the National Trust owns large slices of land around Lancashire. They include the area around Coniston Water, Tarn Hows and the southern end of Windermere in the Lake District; Arnside Knott and Eaves and Waterslack Woods off Morecambe Bay; the Stubbins Estate and Holcombe Moor near Gawthorpe Hall at Padiham; and the sand dunes and woods off the coast at Formby.

THE STAR RESTAURANTS

Despite its wealth of good food, Lancashire, by its modern-day boundaries, has only one restaurant holding a prestigious star from the Michelin inspectors: Northcote Manor near Langho, a few miles from Blackburn and Burnley (tel 01254 240555 or visit www.northcote.com).

In the Furness area – now part of Cumbria but historically part of Lancashire – are two more Michelin-starred restaurants: L'Enclume in Cartmel (tel 015395 36362 or visit www.lenclume.co.uk) and Holbeck Ghyll Country House near Windermere (tel 015394 32375 or visit www.holbeck-ghyll.co.uk).

Four more places in 'real' Lancashire receive a Bib Gourmand from Michelin for 'good food at moderate prices'. They are The Waggon at Bury, The White Hart at Oldham, The Warehouse Brasserie at Southport and Twelve at Thornton Cleveleys.

A LANCASHIRE DICTIONARY PART TWO:
F TO O

A second batch of words from the Lancashire dialect, together with their translations into standard English.

faff to waste time
fain glad
fair very, completely; as in 'fair hungry'
fash to trouble
fause clever, crafty
favour to resemble
fettle to mend; also condition
fizzog face
flay to frighten
flit to run away
fooak folk, people
fost first
front end spring and summer of a year
fuddled drunk
fun' found

gobbin a fool
gone west died
good way a long distance
gormless daft, slow on the uptake
gradely proper, great
grondad grandfather
gronny grandmother

ha'porth a fool; literally halfpenny-worth
hissel' himself
hooam home
hoofed fed up
howsome wholesome

jerry shop ale house
jiggered very tired or broken

jolly robbins fanciful ideas, fiction

keck to tip over
keks trousers
knout cheeky person

lace to hit
lad boy
Lanky Lancashire; also its dialect
lass girl
likely handsome, sharp
limb o' th' devil a mischievous person
lip impudence
lish active
lither lazy
little house outdoor toilet
lumber mischief

mam mother
marlock mischief
maunt must not
mawkin dirty
mebbe maybe
mek do make do, manage
met might
mich much
middlin' OK, neither good nor bad
misel myself
mitch to truant
mither to confuse, bewilder
mollycoddle to indulge
mun must

nay no
nazzy cross
nesh soft, weak or cold
neet night
netty outdoor toilet
nobbut naught but, only
nooan no-one
nowt nothing

o'er over
oon oven
owd old
'owdo how are you?
owt anything
owtelse anything else

A SPOTTER'S GUIDE TO SHEEP

Sheep are an integral part of Lancashire's landscape, shaping the hills and fields of its countryside and providing a major source of income for the county's farmers. Here is a guide to a dozen of the most popular breeds.

Beltex. Medium-sized sheep with large hindquarters and narrow shoulders. It was introduced to the UK from the continent in the 1980s.

Blackface. Probably the most common breed of sheep in the country, found in different cross-breed types from region to region. They have black or black-and-white faces and legs, white fleeces and are always horned.

Blue Faced Leicester. One of the longest and largest breeds in the country, and also one of the best for wool, with consequently high prices. They have long, neat ears, no horns and, as the name suggests, heads that appear to have a blue tinge.

Dalesbred. A hardy breed that is native to the Yorkshire Dales, though it has spread far beyond and has become very popular for cross-breeding. They have black faces with distinctive white patches above the nostrils, and round horns.

Herdwick. Most commonly found in the northern slice of Lancashire in the Lake District, the Herdwick is the hardiest breed of sheep in the country, able to withstand ferocious weather on high, exposed fellsides. Herdwicks have white, docile looking faces and plain cream or grey fleeces that are tough and weatherproof.

Lonk. A large breed of sheep, popular on the Pennines and, like the Herdwick, able to withstand harsh weather and poor grazing conditions. Lonks have mostly white faces with black patches around the nose and eyes, and neat, short, white fleeces.

North of England Mule. Medium-sized hornless sheep with clear wool, brown or white face and a pointy nose. Very easy to rear and care for, making it a popular breed.

Rough Fell. Another strong, resilient upland breed that has been farmed across northern England for centuries. These sheep have large bodies, mostly black heads with white noses, thick, long fleeces and white legs. Rough Fells usually make for very good lamb meat.

Swaledale. Another native of Yorkshire to have crossed the Pennines, this breed joins the Herdwick in being able to cope with tough weather and scant food on the high fells and moors. Swaledales are medium sized with white muzzles, white stripes above each eye, curly, wide horns and thick, long tails. Often crossed with other breeds.

Suffolk. Another very common breed across the UK, this one has an all-black head and legs with contrasting white wool.

Texel. A mostly white sheep with occasional black spots, plus a short neck and crinkled wool. It is a hardy breed that produces excellent meat.

Zwartbles. A rarer breed, having only been introduced to the UK from Holland in the 1980s. They are a tame and docile breed, with no horns and a thick dark fleece with a white blaze.

LANCASHIRE'S SLAVE TRADE

Prosperous periods of industry in Lancashire have usually been overshadowed by the suffering of those whose hard labour enriched a handful of people - but no part of the county's history is remembered with deeper shame than the era of slave trade.

Organised trading of slaves started in Britain in the 1640s, though it wasn't until the 1700s that Lancashire became properly involved through Liverpool, an expanding port with an increasing merchant class. As the 18th century went on it established itself as by some distance the most significant slave trade port in the country, launching at least 5,000 sailings to Africa over the course of a century and, in the two decades before abolition, responsible for more than three quarters of all of Europe's slaving voyages. Further north in the county it was rivalled for a short while by Lancaster, which at its busiest was the fourth largest slaving port behind Liverpool, London and Bristol.

The traders established the 'slave triangle', setting off from ports like Liverpool for West Africa, buying people there or exchanging them for goods, and packing them into their ships for the next leg of the journey – the infamous Middle Passage – to the Caribbean and Americas. Here the slaves were sold and put to work on the plantations, ruled over by British owners with a rod of iron and utter absence of compassion. The ships meanwhile returned to their English ports, laden with exports of slave labour like sugar, coffee, tobacco and cotton.

Liverpool in the 18th century was dominated by slavery-related commerce. Nearly all of the city's merchants and leading citizens had some connection to the trade, and every mayor of the city during the second half of the century was involved in it. But while it was more tightly wound up with the slave trade than anywhere else in Europe, Lancashire was part of the campaign to end it, too. One of the largest petitions against slavery was compiled in Manchester in 1788 and signed by 10,000 people – one in five of the city's residents at the time. Liverpool also submitted its own smaller petition, and it was here that abolitionists like Thomas Clarkson gathered much of their evidence for the campaign against slavery. The growing Quaker movement, particularly strong in Lancashire, also came out against slavery.

The last slave ship left Liverpool in 1807 after abolitionists like Clarkson and William Wilberforce pushed through a law to abolish slave trading. But the transport of already indentured slaves continued until they were finally freed by a further act in 1833 and even, by some particularly unscrupulous owners, beyond. Liverpool and other cities and towns across Lancashire also went on enjoying the benefits of trade links that were indirectly but significantly linked to slavery – either because the slave ship owners bought and carried their exports down to Africa or because they returned with the raw materials that fuelled industries. The import of raw cotton across the Atlantic, for instance, was crucial to Lancashire's textile industry long after the slave trading ended.

Reminders of the slave trade can be found all over Lancashire. The wealth that it generated helped the cities, quaysides, individuals and other industries to flourish, and countless homes built with slave money remain, both in Liverpool and further afield, notably in the southern Lake District. Plenty of streets owe their names to the trade, and some Liverpudlians can trace slave ancestors who found themselve s transported back to Britain to work and live.

Helping Liverpool come to terms with its slavery associations is the excellent International Slavery Museum on Albert Dock, a quayside that was built after abolition but which is nevertheless evocative of the trade after a tour of the exhibitions inside. It is open every day except Christmas and free to enter (tel 0151 478 4499 or visit www.liverpoolmuseums.org.uk/ism).

Perhaps the most poignant memorial to the slave trade can be found at Sunderland Point at the mouth of the Lune Estuary near Lancaster. Here, in the 1730s, a captured young slave from West Africa was held for a while and died, perhaps because of an illness sustained on the long journey. He was buried on unconsecrated ground close to the water, to which a memorial plaque was added 60 years later. The spot has been carefully tended and decorated ever since, and has become something of a local focal point for guilt and grief over Lancashire's associations with slavery.

SOME TWIN TOWNS

What do Le Mans in northern France and Zhaoqing in southern China have in common? Or Los Angeles in the US and St Petersburg in Russia? Not much, except they are all twin towns or cities of places in Lancashire – in these cases Bolton and Manchester.

There are all sorts of reasons why towns and cities seek twinning agreements: international friendship, commercial links, exchange pro grammes for students and perhaps the opportunity for local councilors to jet off to warmer climes for a few days. Most twinning partnerships are struck with locations of a similar size in continental Europe, commonly France or Germany, but some Lancashire towns have looked further afield. Garstang, for instance, is twinned with New Koforidua in Ghana, as a result of its efforts to become the world's first fair-trade town, while Rochdale's Pakistan-born population led it to links with Sahiwal in the Punjab province. Chorley is paired with Székesfehérvár in Hungary, a place easier to visit than it is to pronounce.

This list shows some of the county's interesting twins, including partnerships that are known by other names like sister cities or friendship agreements.

Town	Twin
Ashton-under-Lyme	Chaumont, France
Blackburn	Peronne, France
Blackpool	Bottrop, Germany
Bolton	Le Mans, France; Paderborn, Germany; Zhaoqing, China
Burnley	Vitry-sur-Seine, France
Bury	Angouleme and Tulle, France; Datong, China; Schorndorf, Germany; Woodbury, US
Carnforth	Sailly-sur-la-Lys, France
Chorley	Székesfehérvár, Hungary
Clitheroe	Rivesaltes, France
Dalton-in-Furness	Dalton, US
Droylsden	Villemomble, France
Dunkinfield	Champagnole, France
Fleetwood	Fleetwood, US
Garstang	New Koforidua, Ghana; Media, US
Kirkham	Ancenis, France; Bad Brückenau, Germany
Knowsley	Moers, Germany
Lancaster	Perpignan, France; Rendsburg, Germany; Aalborg, Denmark; Lublin, Poland; Växjö, Sweden
Liverpool	Cologne, Germany; Dublin, Ireland; Shanghai, China
Manchester	Los Angeles, US; Wuhan, China; St Petersburg, Russia
Oldham	Geestacht and Landsberg am Lech, Germany; Kranj, Slovenia
Oswaldtwistle	Falkenberg, Sweden
Preston	Almelo, Netherlands; Nimes, France; Recklinghausen, Germany; Kalisz, Poland
Rochdale	Bielefeld, Germany; Lviv, Ukraine; Sahiwal, Pakistan; Tourcoing and Peine, France
Rossendale	Bocholt, Germany
Salford	Clermont-Ferrand, Narbonne and Saint-Ouen, France; Lünen, Germany
Sefton	Fort Lauderdale, US; Gdansk, Poland; Mons, Belgium
St Helens	Stuttgart, Germany; Chalon-sur-Saône, France
Ulverston	Albert, France
Warrington	Hilden, Germany; Lake County, US; Náchod, Czech Republic
Wigan	Angers, France

ACTORS FROM LANCASHIRE

30 of the best known actors born in Lancashire, together with their home towns.

Caroline Aherne (Wythenshawe)
Tom Baker (Liverpool)
Warren Clarke (Chorlton-cum-Hardy)
Bernard Cribbins (Oldham)
Christopher Eccleston (Salford)
Gracie Fields (Rochdale)
Albert Finney (Salford)
Anna Friel (Rochdale)
Rex Harrison (Houghton)
Bernard Hill (Manchester)
Thora Hird (Morecambe)
Jane Horrocks (Rawtenstall)
John Inman (Blackpool)
Glenda Jackson (Liverpool)
Sue Johnston (Warrington)

Burt Kwouk (Manchester)
Sarah Lancashire (Oldham)
Ian McKellen (Burnley)
Ian McShane (Blackburn)
Jonathan Morris (Urmston)
Derek Nimmo (Liverpool)
Maxine Peake (Blackburn)
Pat Phoenix (Manchester)
Pete Postlethwaite (Warrington)
Robert Powell (Salford)
Leonard Rossiter (Liverpool)
Alison Steadman (Liverpool)
John Thaw (Manchester)
John Thomson (Manchester)
Ricky Tomlinson (Blackpool)

THE STARS OF LANCASHIRE'S CRICKET LEAGUES

Lancashire has always been one of English cricket's heartlands, and while followers' attention is usually on the fortunes of the county side, its club leagues are hugely popular too. Aside from the local rivalries between towns and villages, part of the appeal is the system of professionals, whereby each club is allowed to appoint one paid player each season – very often a recognised star and usually the dominant force in their club's performance that season. The leagues were particularly popular in the county's old mill and factory towns, where work would end at noon on Saturdays in time for workers to watch an afternoon's cricket, and where the tradition of the paid pro endures most strongly.

When the system began in the late 19th century it was common to engage English players, their fees raised from paying spectators. Later, as overseas players became more widely known, clubs started to hire big names from abroad – in the 1970s and 1980s often from the world's best side, the West Indies, and more recently from Australia,

South Africa and Asia. From the hundreds of players to have passed through Lancashire's various leagues, here are 25 of the best, together with the clubs they represented.

Allan Border, Australia (East Lancs)
Chris Cairns, New Zealand (Bacup)
Ian Chappell, Australia (Ramsbottom)
Michael Clarke, Australia (Ramsbottom)
Learie Constantine, West Indies (Nelson)
Kapil Dev, India (Nelson)
Allan Donald, South Africa (Rishton)
Andy Flower, Zimbabwe (Crimble)
Joel Garner, West Indies (Littleborough)
Jason Gillespie, Australia (Rishton)
Wes Hall, West Indies (Accrington)
George Headley, West Indies (Haslingden)
Michael Holding, West Indies (Rishton)
Dennis Lillee, Australia (Haslingden)
Ray Lindwall, Australia (Nelson)
Clive Lloyd, West Indies (Haslingden)
Colin Miller, Australia (Rawtenstall)
Viv Richards, West Indies (Rishton)
Andy Roberts, West Indies (Haslingden)
Garfield Sobers, West Indies (Radcliffe)
Mark Taylor, Australia (Greenmount)
Clyde Walcott, West Indies (Enfield)
Shane Warne, Australia (Accrington)
Steve Waugh, Australia (Nelson)
Everton Weekes, West Indies (Bacup)

LANCASHIRE FOOD –
FISH AND CHIPS

Although Yorkshire might have something to say about it, Lancashire likes to consider itself the home of fish and chips.

The county certainly has all the ingredients of a successful chippy – an easy supply of fresh fish via its coastline and ports, plentiful potatoes that are considered locally to be the best in Britain, and a hard-working and hungry population. In fact, a survey by seafood marketing agency Seafish found that Lancashire has more fish and chip shops per capita than any other part of the country – one for every 914 residents. Between them, they sell some 20 million portions of fish and chips a year.

Early versions of the meal were sold from fried fish warehouses, at first usually with baked or boiled potatoes or bread, and Charles Dickens refers to one such place in *Oliver Twist*. A few years later, someone had the bright idea of serving fish with chips, and the combination stuck. Cheap, filling and quickly obtained, it became particularly popular among Lancashire's industrial working class, and fish and chip shops sprung up across the county's mill towns. When workers started to go on holiday, to resorts like Blackpool and Morecambe, more outlets quickly opened to serve them. Fish and chips has been associated with the seaside ever since.

Although it is universally popular, the meal is the subject of considerable trans-Pennine rivalry. While Yorkshire claims the oldest surviving shop – in Yeadon near Leeds – Lancashire boasts the first one to open, in the market at Mossley near Oldham on the eastern fringes of the county in 1863. Both counties naturally consider their versions to be superior, though they do at least agree that servings in the north of England are far superior to those in the south.

Fish and chip culture certainly varies around the country. While the south generally cooks cod and has lately added fancier fish like hake or skate, Lancashire and Yorkshire tend to fry haddock, and while ketchup might be served with chips beneath the Watford Gap, above it they come with gravy. Some things about fish and chips change – it is now served in plastic trays rather than wrapped in old newspapers, for instance – but Lancashire remains hugely loyal to its favourite takeaway.

Ten humorously named fish and chip shops in Lancashire

Chip Ahoy, Blackpool

The Codfather, St Annes

The Contented Sole, Preston

The Frying Squad, Blackpool

The Happy Haddock, Preston

Joyce's Plaice, Fleetwood

Northern Sole, St Annes

Ocean's Eleven, Leigh

Oh My Cod, Rawtenstall

Something Fishy, Bacup

THE COUNTRYSIDE CODE

There are five main points of the Countryside Code, which was first drawn up by the Commons and Open Spaces Society in the 1930s and revised into its current form by the Countryside Agency – now Natural England – in 2004. It helps members of the public respect, protect and enjoy their natural surroundings in Lancashire and beyond.

Be safe – plan ahead and follow any signs
Leave gates and property as you find them
Protect plants and animals, and take your litter home
Keep dogs under close control
Consider other people

GREAT LANCASTRIANS –
L.S. LOWRY

Even the most loyal of admirers would probably admit that Lancashire has produced more technically gifted artists than L.S. Lowry. But few painters have developed so distinctive and instantly recognisable a style – and none chronicled the industrial Lancashire of the first half of the 20th century half so memorably.

Laurence Stephen Lowry was born in 1887 in Manchester. After a fairly unhappy upbringing as an only child, he started work as an office clerk at 16, using some of his wages to take evening art classes. In his late twenties he won places at art schools in Manchester and Salford and, after several years of education and practice, achieved his first exhibitions, sales and commissions in the early 1920s.

Lowry's family had lived in some of Manchester's leafier suburbs, but financial problems led them to move in 1909 to Pendlebury, then a town north of Salford that was dominated by mills and collieries. At first he disliked the industrial landscape, but it interested him more and more as he grew older and he stayed in Pendlebury for nearly 40 years. The motifs of his paintings – pallid skies, high-rise factories and tenements, belching chimneys, large crowds of indistinct figures hunched against the cold – were inspired by what he saw, here and in other industrial Lancashire towns.

The scenes, coupled with what is sometimes called a primitive style, make Lowry's paintings instantly recognisable as his. But while his matchstick men were certainly the result of a simple approach to art, Lowry was a far more considered and knowledgeable artist than he is often given credit for. He was a huge admirer of the pre-Raphaelite, Impressionist and Expressionist movements among others, and painted portraits, still lifes and country scenes too. As Lancashire's industrial powerhouses started to wane in the 1950s, he moved even further away from the subject that, by now, he was closely associated with. In all, he completed around a thousand paintings and many more drawings – some refined to exhibition standard and others simply sketches on the backs of envelopes or napkins.

Lowry was recognised in his lifetime by art awards, honorary degrees and the freedom of Salford, though he turned down an OBE, CBE and knighthood – making him, so far as is known, the person to have turned down the most official honours in a lifetime. But while he was certainly very popular towards the end of his life he was not, by the standards of most renowned artists, a rich man, and continued in his office job until his sixties. Instead, his reputation soared long after his peak output as an artist, through retrospectives and, perhaps, a nostalgia for the lost industrial north. His work now often changes hands for seven figure sums, and an auction in 2007 sold one of his paintings – of mill workers celebrating a rare holiday – for £3.8 million.

The best place to find out more about Lowry's life and work is the arts and entertainment centre named after him on Salford Quays. Opened in 2000, it features around 400 of his pieces – the largest number anywhere – and a Lowry Archive, housed among 21,530 square feet (2,000 sq m) of performance spaces, galleries and cafés (tel 0870 787 5780 or visit www.thelowry.com). There is a statue of Lowry, sat on a bench with sketchbook in hand, in Mottram, a village east of Manchester and just outside Lancashire's borders where he lived for his last 30 years.

THE LANCASHIRE BRAND

What does Lancashire mean to you? When the county's tourist agency did some research into how it is perceived, it got lots of different answers and some confusion among visitors about its values and strengths. So like all good marketing professionals must, it set to work on building the Lancashire brand. The results included two slogans for promoting Lancashire further afield: 'The home of the good things in life' and 'Where life feels good'.

Beyond that, Visit Lancashire identified five core brand values for the area: 'closeness', in physical and emotional terms; 'realness', meaning proper food and fun and people without pretension; 'traditional quality', with everything done properly; 'genuine warmth' and the essence of northerness; and 'big wows and little wows', intended to indicate that Lancashire offers lots of small pleasures as well as large-scale attractions. Marketing jargon or an accurate reflection of Lancashire's appeal? Visitor numbers are steadily increasing, so perhaps the agency's branding has, along with its other promotional schemes, had a positive effect.

LANCASHIRE'S CATHEDRALS

By their definition as the seat of a bishop, Lancashire has three of the Church of England's 42 cathedrals. They are:

Blackburn Cathedral. There has been a church on this town-centre site for more than a thousand years, but it was only designated a cathedral in 1926 and consecrated at the end of building work in the 1970s.

Liverpool Cathedral. When the position of Bishop of Liverpool was created in 1880, the city didn't have a cathedral proper. So after a popular architectural competition, Giles Gilbert Scott designed what was to become - more than 70 years later - the world's fifth largest cathedral, nearly 660 feet (200 m) long and with a tower reaching up 328 feet (100 m).

Manchester Cathedral. Churches have come and gone on the cathedral's site since Norman and perhaps even Saxon times, but most of the current building dates from the 19th century. It obtained cathedral status in 1847 and received large-scale refurbishment over 20 years after being hit by a German bomb in the Second World War. An IRA bomb caused further damage in 1996.

The Roman Catholic Church has three cathedrals in Lancashire: the Cathedral Church of St John the Evangelist in Salford, consecrated in 1850; St Peter's Cathedral in Lancaster, consecrated in 1859; and Liverpool Metropolitan Cathedral, consecrated in 1967.

LANCASHIRE'S BOOKER WINNER

Of the 41 authors to have won the Booker Prize, the most prestigious award for fiction in the UK and Commonwealth, only one was born in Lancashire. He was J.G. (James Gordon) Farrell, who was born in Liverpool in 1935 and educated at the Rossall private school, near Cleveleys on the Lancashire coast. He became the fifth Booker winner in 1973 for his book *The Siege of Krishnapur*, part of his 'Empire' trilogy that explored the fallout of British colonial rule, and used his acceptance speech to criticise the then sponsors of the prize. Farrell died in 1979 at the age of 44, drowned while out fishing in Ireland.

Lancashire has also produced the author with the most places on the Booker Prize's shortlists in the four decades since it was launched. Beryl Bainbridge, born in Liverpool and raised a little way up the coast in Formby, has been shortlisted five times, in 1973, 1974, 1990, 1996 and 1998, without ever going on to win the award.

SOME PLACE NAMES AND THEIR MEANINGS: A TO M

60 large and small Lancashire places, and how they got their names.

Accrington – Farmstead or village where acorns are found or stored. It probably derives from the nearby forest of Rossendale, where pigs ate acorns

Adlington – Associated with someone called Eadwulf or similar Old English name

Aigburth – Oak tree hill

Aintree – A solitary tree

Ashton – Settlement were ash trees grow. There are several Ashtons in Lancashire

Atherton – Farmstead or village of Aethelhere or similar Old English name

Bacup – The valley by a ridge

Bamber Bridge – Origins are uncertain, but it could derive from the bridge of Bimme or similar Old English name

Bardsea – The island of Beorda or similar name

Barrow-in-Furness – Island with a promontory. The town took its name from a nearby island. Furness means headland by the rump-shaped island

Baxenden - Valley where flat stones for baking are found

Bickerstaffe - The river bank or landing place belonging to bee-keepers

Blackburn - Black or dark stream. It takes its name from the River Blackwater

Blackpool - Black or dark pool, unsurprisingly. It refers to the pool that drained Marton Mere

Bolton - Settlement with a special building. It is a common place name in northern England, used to distinguish proper settlements from their surrounding land

Bootle - Special dwelling

Bowland - Area of land in a bow, possibly referring to a bend in a river

Brierfield - Field where briers grow

Broughton - Farmstead or village by a stream. There are several Broughtons across Lancashire

Burnley - Woodland clearing by the River Brun

Burscough - Wood by a fortified place

Bury - Place of a fort or stronghold

Carnforth - The ford of cranes or herons

Cartmel - Sandbank by rocky ground

Chipping - Marketplace

Chorley - Clearing of freemen, derived from the Old English *ceorl* for the rank of freeman

Clitheroe - Hill of loose stones. Taken from the hill on which the castle stands

Colne - Origins are uncertain, though it was probably derived from a river that once ran here

Coniston - The king's settlement or manor

Dalton - Estate or enclosure in a valley. Lancashire has several Daltons

Darwen - Takes its name from the river, meaning where oak trees grow

Droylesden - Valley of the dry stream

Eccles - Church, from the Celtic *egles*

Entwistle - The fork in the river frequented by ducks

Everton - Farmstead or village with pigs or boar

Fleetwood - Named after the town's founder, Sir Peter Hesketh Fleetwood

Formby - Homestead belonging to Forni or similar Scandinavian name

Garstang - Pole shaped like a spear, probably used to mark a boundary

Goosnargh - The hill-pasture of Gosan or similar name, probably Irish or Scandinavian in origin

Great Harwood - Probably the hares' wood. The Great was added to differentiate it from other Harwoods

Grizedale - Valley where pigs are kept

Hale – Low-lying nooks of land by a river

Halton – Farmstead or settlement in the bend of a river, in this case the Lune

Haslingden – Valley where hazel trees grow

Hawkshead – Hill pasture of Haukr or similar Scandinavian name

Haydock – The place of wheat and barley

Heaton – Farmstead on high land

Heysham – Homestead or village in the wood

Hornby – Farmstead or village on a horn-shaped piece of land

Hulme – Island or dry ground in the marsh

Ireby – Settlement of the Irish

Kirkby and **Kirkham** – Village with a church

Lancaster – The Roman fort on the River Lune. Lancashire is derived from Lancastershire, meaning district of Lancaster

Leigh – A place in the woodland clearing

Leyland – Area of fallow land

Liverpool – Pool with thick or muddied water

Lytham – A place on the slopes, probably referring to the sand dunes along the coast

Manchester – The Roman fort at Mamucio, a name possibly derived from the Celtic for breast-shaped hill

Morecambe – Takes its name from the Bay on which it sits, meaning the curved inlet

LANCASHIRE INDUSTRY – COTTON

The rise and fall of the cotton business over the last few hundred years is, in many ways, the story of Lancashire. Certainly no other industry has left so great a mark on the county – for better or for worse.

Prior to the Industrial Revolution, textile production was largely a cottage industry, with families making their own clothes in the home on handlooms and perhaps selling on whatever extra items they were able to turn out. But as demand increased and the means emerged to drive spinning machines, factories began to spring up. Those running them soon discovered that powered production made for massively increased efficiency and output than human labour alone.

Factory manufacture transformed not just cotton production and working habits, but life. Many of those who previously spun for themselves in rural Lancashire now went to work in massive, strictly regimented mills and warehouses in Manchester and the satellite towns around it. Men, women and children alike slaved away for twelve hours a day, six days a week, in stiflingly hot and humid conditions, the air thick with damaging cotton dust and ringing with the deafening sound of rows of unreliable machines that frequently inflicted horrific accidents.

Life wasn't much better at home. Housing in the cotton towns was thrown up fast and without much care for residents' comfort, space or sanitation, leading to chronic overcrowding and rife disease. A new industrial working class was created, poor and vulnerable but increasingly unionised and restless. With some honourable exceptions, mill owners ruled them with a rod of iron, though workers' pressure and parliamentary reform from the middle of the 19th century did slowly start to reduce child labour, shorten working hours and improve housing conditions. While workers toiled in virtual slavery, life for their employers was very different, and the houses they built with the vast wealth earned from cotton can still be seen around Lancashire and beyond.

While across the county borders Yorkshire was making itself the centre for wool production, Lancashire's mill workers soon established their county as the world capital of cotton. It owed its success partly to its climate, with enough water in the rivers to power the mills and enough dampness in the air to maintain the moisture in fragile cotton yarns; and partly to its steady supply of labour. The industry grew to such an extent that by 1825, raw cotton was the country's largest import. Entire towns were now dedicated to cotton, with the 'cottonopolis' of Manchester the headquarters for its trade. By 1860, Lancashire had more than two thousand mills, employing a third of a million people.

After a century of growth came several years of crisis, when the American Civil War led to a blockade on the shipping of raw cotton from the plantations in the southern states. Coupled with excessive production in the boom years that had reduced demand, the cotton famine put more than half of Lancashire's mill workers out of work, forcing them to rely on charitable or poor law relief. It wasn't until 1865 that the industry recovered, and it now grew again, to a peak in the early 1910s when Britain's output reached 7 or 8 billion square yards of cloth a year. But other countries, notably Japan, were starting to catch up, turning out cheaper and better materials more efficiently, and the First World War tightened the brakes on Lancashire's production.

After the war, the depression set the cotton mills on a steady but sure decline. By 1958 Britain was a net importer of cotton – an unthinkable situation a few decades earlier – and through the 1960s, Lancashire's mills closed their gates at the rate of one a week. Though textile production continued – and continues – in the northwest, by the 1980s the cotton industry had gone. Cities like Manchester were by now diversified enough to adjust to life after cotton, but towns like Blackburn, Oldham and Burnley were decimated, their vast empty factories a reminder of past glories.

Most of Lancashire's mills have now been demolished or renovated, turned into flats or workspaces for new industries. But a few have been preserved or adapted into museums celebrating the county's era of King Cotton. The best places to find out more include the Helmshore Mills Textile Museum in Rossendale (tel 01706 226459 or visit www.lancashire.gov.uk); the Lewis Museum of Textile Machinery in Blackburn (tel 01254 667130 or visit www.blackburn.gov.uk); the Queen Street Mill Textile Museum (tel 01282 412555 or visit www.lancashire.gov.uk); and the Park Bridge Industrial Hamlet in Ashton-under-Lyne (tel 0161 330 9613 or visit www.ashton-under-lyne.com).

20 major mill towns of Lancashire

Accrington	Leigh
Ashton-under-Lyne	Nelson
Bacup	Oldham
Blackburn	Oswaldtwistle
Bolton	Padiham
Burnley	Preston
Bury	Ramsbottom
Colne	Rochdale
Darwen	Royton
Heywood	Wigan

TEN HAUNTED PLACES

Whether or not you give any credence to supernatural theories, Lancashire has certainly had its fair share of reports of ghostly sightings and strange goings-on. Perhaps because of its rich history and abundance of stately homes and other old buildings, this part of the country is rated very highly by ghost hunters and mediums. Here are ten of the most interesting haunted places and their stories.

Chingle Hall, Goosnargh. This manor house, with original 13th-century elements intact, was once claimed to be England's most haunted house. It was a sanctuary for Catholics in times of persecution and has a long roll call of ghosts including several martyred Saints. It used to run overnight ghost vigils but is now privately owned.

Claife Heights, near Windermere. The wooded slopes of the western shores of Windermere, making up the far fringes of Lancashire, are said to be home to the spirit of a monk from Furness Abbey, sent mad with grief after being rejected by one of the fallen women he rescued. A local priest exorcised him after several sightings and dispatched him to a quarry, marked on Ordnance Survey maps in his honour as *Crier of Claife*.

Lancaster Castle. The cells and hanging rooms here are supposedly haunted by numerous prisoners of the past, including the Pendle witches. The building is still a court and a prison but good access is available seven days a week; even if you've no interest in ghosts, a tour here is an unsettling experience.

Punch Bowl, Hurst Green. This cosy Ribble Valley pub is apparently haunted by Ned King, a feared local highwayman who liked to drink there until he was arrested and hanged on a nearby hill.

Rufford Old Hall, near Ormskirk. The ghost is a woman who pined away here in the 16th century after her soldier lover was killed while away fighting. Visitors to the National Trust-owned property occasionally report sightings and mysterious sounds, smells and sensations.

Samlesbury Hall, near Preston. Advertises itself as one of the country's most haunted houses in order to promote its regular ghost tours and paranormal investigations. Residents include the White Lady, a woman whose lover was murdered by her own family, and a priest beheaded during the Reformation.

Smithills Hall, Bolton. Features the ghost of preacher George Marsh, tried for heresy during Mary Tudor's reign then burned at the stake, plus sundry other spirits.

The Sun Inn, Chipping. Lancashire's self-styled most haunted pub with the ghost of Lizzie Dean, a 19th-century maid who hanged herself after being jilted by a man.

Towneley Hall, Burnley. The several ghosts here include the restless spirit of Sir John Towneley, wracked with guilt after he forced tenants off his land; the soldiers of Oliver Cromwell sent to arrest a Royalist sympathiser; and, of course, the ubiquitous and mysterious White Lady.

Wardley Hall, Worsley. This medieval manor house contains
the skull of St Ambrose, a Catholic martyr hung, drawn and
quartered in 1641. Strange things apparently happen whenever
the skull has been removed in the past, so it is now housed
securely behind glass. The hall is the official residence of the
Bishop of Salford.

⊗⊗ ⊗⊗ ⊗⊗ ⊗⊗ ⊗⊗ ⊗⊗ ⊗⊗ ⊗⊗ ⊗⊗ ⊗⊗ ⊗⊗ ⊗⊗

LANCASHIRE POEMS
'COME WHOAM TO THY CHILDER AN' ME'

Of Lancashire's many dialect poets over the centuries, Edwin Waugh
is probably the most respected, and this his most famous work. Born in
Rochdale in 1817, he worked from the age of 12 as an apprentice to
a printer and bookseller and soon became interested in writing. But
it wasn't until publication of 'Come Whoam To Thy Childer An' Me' in a
Manchester newspaper in 1856 that he became widely known and was
able to work full-time as a writer.

The poem begins with a Lancashire woman imploring her husband
to return home to his family, and ends happily with the errant man
promising to do so. In expressive dialect and full of sentimentality,
it was hugely popular in Lancashire at the time, and remains treasured
by those, including the Edwin Waugh Dialect Society, who strive to
preserve the local dialect.

Aw've just mended th' fire wi' a cob;
Owd Swaddle has brought thi' new shoon;
There's some nice bacon-collops o'th hob
An' a quart o' ale posset i'th oon.
Aw've brought thi top coat, doesto know
For th' rain's comin' deawn very dree;
An th' har'stone's as white as new snow –
Come whoam to thy childer an' me.

When aw put little Sally to bed,
Hoo cried 'cos her feyther weren't theer,
So aw kiss'd th' little thing, an aw said
Thae'd bring her a ribbon fro' th' fair;
An' aw gave her a doll an some rags
An' a nice little white cotton-bo'
An' aw kiss'd her again; but hoo said
'At hoo wanted to kiss thee an' o'.

An' Dick, too, aw'd sich wark wi' him,
   Afore aw could get him up stairs;
Thae towd him thae'd bring him a drum,
He said, when he were sayin' his prayers
Then he looked i' my face, an' he said,
   "Has th' boggarts taen houd o' my dad?"
An' he cried till his e'en were quite red –
   He likes thee some weel, does yon lad!

At th' lung-length, aw geet 'em laid still;
   An' aw hearken'd t' folks' feet 'at went by;
So aw iron't o' my clooas reet well,
   An' aw hanged 'em o' th maiden to dry;
When aw'd mended thy stockins an' shirts,
   Aw sit deawn to knit i' my cheer,
An' aw rayley did feel rayther hurt –
   Mon, aw'm onely when theaw arrn't theer.

"Aw've a drum an' a trumpet for Dick;
   Aw've a yard o' blue ribbon for Sal;
Aw've a book full o' babs, an' a stick
   An' some baccy an' pipes for mysel';
Aw've brought thee some coffee an' tay;
   Iv thae'll feel i' my pocket, tha'll see;
An' aw've bought tho a new cap today –
   But Aw al'ays brings summat for thee!

"God bless tho', my lass; aw'll go whoam,
   An' aw'll kiss thee an' th' childer o' round;
Thae knows, that wherever aw roam,
   Aw'm fain to get back to th' owd ground;
Aw can do wi' a crack o'er a glass;
   Aw can do wi' a bit of a spree;
But aw've no gradely comfort, my lass,
   Except wi' yon childer and thee."

Glossary: *cob* (line 1) means coal; *shoon* (2) means shoes; *collops* (3) means slices; *oon* (4) means oven; *dree* (6) means continuously; *har'stone* (7) means hearth stone; *cotton-bo'* (14) means cotton ball; *o'* (16) means all; *boggarts* (22) means ghosts or evil spirits; *e'en* (23) means eyes; *lung-length* (25) means end; *onely* (32) means lonely; *babs* (35) means babies; *tay* (37) means tea; *fain* (44) means glad; *crack* (45) means talk; and *gradely* (47) means proper.

THE KING'S SIRLOIN

One of Lancashire's most frequently repeated folk tales is the story of how King James I came to christen the sirloin steak in the county. The story runs that the King, staying at Hoghton Tower in 1617, spotted an exceptionally large joint of beef on his feast table and, in an uncharacteristic display of wit, rose with his sword and knighted it on the spot with the words 'Arise Sir Loin'.

Unfortunately, however, the story is almost certainly apocryphal, the word having existed for several hundred years before James made his little joke. Rather, sirloin probably derives from the Old French term *sur la longe*, meaning 'above the loin'. The tale was probably invented by a punning writer of James' time or afterwards, and it has been credited to several other monarchs, too, including those with famously healthy appetites like Henry VIII.

BLACKPOOL IN NUMBERS

16,000,000 . . . . estimated annual visits made to Blackpool

£45,000,000 . . . . . estimated annual income from the tourist industry

2,000,000 . . . . estimated number of postcards sent each year

90,636 . . . . beds for holidaymakers in hotels, B&Bs and other serviced accommodation

1863 . . . . year Blackpool's first pier – the North – opened

1879 . . . . year the first Illuminations were lit

1885 . . . . year the Tramway opened

1894 . . . . year both the Tower and Grand Theatre opened

1905 . . . . year the Promenade opened

518 . . . . height in feet (158 m) of the Tower

9 . . . . tons of paint needed to paint the Tower

1 . . . . . inch (2.5 cm) the Tower sways in a wind of 70 miles per hour

11.25 . . . . length in miles (18 km) of the Tramway line

61 . . . . stops on the line

220 . . . . height in feet (67 m) of Blackpool's Old Big Wheel, in its time the world's biggest. It closed in 1928

108 . . . . height in feet (33 m) of the New Big Wheel on Central Pier

11,000,000 . . . . estimated number of coins put into North Pier arcades each year

8 . . . . arc lamps in the first display of Blackpool's Illuminations

22 . . . . weeks it now takes to put up the Illuminations

9 . . . . weeks it takes to take them down again

6 . . . . length in miles (10 km) of the Illuminations

66 . . . . nights for which the Illuminations remain lit each year

711 . . . . weight in tons of the Illuminations equipment

960,000 . . . . . units of electricity used by the Illuminations each year

1,900,000 . . . . cost in pounds of the annual display

3,500,000 . . . . visitors the Illuminations are estimated to draw to Blackpool each year

45 . . . . staff working full-time on the Illuminations, including electricians, mechanics, engineers and artists

7,800,000 . . . . visitors to Blackpool Pleasure Beach each year

125 . . . . rides and attractions at the Beach

236 . . . . height in feet (72 m) of its biggest rollercoaster, the Pepsi Max Big One

74 . . . . maximum speed in miles per hour (119 kmh) of the rollercoaster

3 . . . . duration in minutes of a ride

500,000 . . . . estimated number of candyflosses sold each year at the beach

47 . . . . estimated miles (76 km) worth of hotdogs sold each year

LANCASHIRE'S WORLD HERITAGE SITE

Given its natural and cultural riches, it is perhaps surprising that Lancashire has only one of the UK's 27 World Heritage Sites, designated by UNESCO as being of particular international significance and worthy of special protection. For its importance in maritime mercantile history, that site is Liverpool – or, more specifically, six areas in the city's centre and docklands. The honour reognises Liverpool's history as one of the world's biggest trading centres in the 18th and 19th centuries, and also its role in advancing technologies and methods in docks and transport systems during that time.

Despite the massive changes to the city since its golden era of trading, Liverpool's docks and commercial areas have been very well preserved, and will continue to be thanks to their World Heritage status. The six areas recognised by UNESCO are the Pier Head, the Albert Dock and the four conservation areas of the Stanley Dock, Duke Street, the Commercial Quarter around Castle Street and the Cultural Quarter around William Brown Street.

LANCASHIRE'S BREWERIES

Lancashire has a long and proud tradition of brewing, and while some of the big beer companies that once had headquarters in the county have now ceased production or moved elsewhere, they have been replaced by plenty of small start-ups. There are now around fifty breweries in Lancashire, as measured by its traditional boundaries, ranging from tiny hobby breweries to large brands like Cains in Liverpool and Daniel Thwaites in Blackburn. Some of these breweries offer tours to anyone wanting to find out more about the beer-making process, and some are bottling their beers for sale beyond Lancashire. And encouraged by a renaissance of real ale drinking, more are springing up every year. Here are Lancashire's breweries:

Allgates Brewery, Wigan
Banktop Brewery, Bolton
Bazens' Brewery, Salford
Boggart Hole Clough Brewery, Manchester
The Bowland Brewery, Clitheroe
Brysons Brewery, Morecambe
Robert Cain Brewery, Liverpool
Cambrinus Craft Brewery, Prescot
Coach House Brewing Company, Warrington
Coniston Brewing Company, Coniston
Cumbrian Legendary Ales, Hawkshead
Fallons Exquisite Ales, Darwen
Foxfield Brewery, Broughton-in-Furness
Fuzzy Duck Brewery, Poulton-le-Fylde
Garthela Brewhouse, Blackburn
Green Mill Brewery, Rochdale
Hart Brewery, Little Eccleston
Higsons Brewery, Liverpool

Joseph Holt Brewery, Manchester
Hopstar Brewery, Darwen
Hornbeam Brewery, Manchester
Hydes Brewery, Manchester
Kirkby Lonsdale Brewery, Kirkby Lonsdale
Lancaster Brewery, Lancaster
J.W. Lees, Manchester
Leyden Brewing, Bury
Liverpool Organic Brewery, Liverpool
Lytham Brewery, Lytham
Marble Brewery, Manchester
Mayflower Brewery, Wigan
Moonstone Brewery, Burnley
Moorhouses Brewery, Burnley
Outstanding Brewing Company, Bury
Pennine Ale, Haslingden
Phoenix Brewery, Heywood
Pictish Brewery, Rochdale
Prospect Brewery, Wigan
Red Rose Brewery, Great Harwood
Southport Brewery, Southport
Stringers Beer, Ulverston
Abraham Thompson, Barrow
Three B's Brewery, Blackburn
Daniel Thwaites Brewery, Blackburn
Ulverston Brewing Company, Ulverston
Wapping Brewery, Liverpool
George Wright Brewing Company, Rainford

LANCASHIRE ON TV

The cities and countryside of Lancashire have been very popular with TV producers over the years. Long-running series like *Coronation Street* and *Brookside* have been set and filmed here, but so too have a rich variety of dramas and sitcoms, making it perhaps TV's second capital after London. Here are 25 of the best known programmes to have been at least partly filmed here.

Coronation Street (1960 onwards)
Britain's longest running TV soap, firmly set and filmed in Lancashire, on Granada's purpose-built Manchester set.

Z-Cars (1962 to 1978)
Long-running police drama set in the fictional town of Newtown but closely based on Kirkby in Merseyside.

Juliet Bravo (1980 to 1985)
Set in the Lancashire town of Hartley, and filmed partly at Bacup police station as well as locations over the border in Yorkshire.

Brookside (1982 to 2003)
Long-running and increasingly implausible TV soap that was filmed in a purpose-built cul-de-sac of houses in Liverpool.

Bread (1986 to 1991)
Popular, sentimental sitcom-soap crossover that was set and filmed in Liverpool, especially in the suburb of Dingle.

Oranges are Not the Only Fruit (1990)
Classic BBC drama filmed in Accrington and Rawtenstall in Lancashire, as well as in Yorkshire.

Cracker (1993 to 2006)
Set in Manchester and largely filmed at locations in and around the city, including Didsbury and Longsight.

Common as Muck (1994 to 1997)
Comedy series about binmen filmed in Oldham.

Moll Flanders (1996)
BBC bodice-ripper with scenes shot at Hoghton Tower near Preston, Astley Hall in Chorley and Rivington Castle on the west Pennine Moors.

Cold Feet (1998 to 2003)
Popular comedy drama set in Manchester and filmed in and around the city and further south into Cheshire.

The Royle Family (1998 to 2008)
Acclaimed comedy set almost entirely in a house in
Wythenshawe, where co-creator Caroline Aherne grew up,
though filmed in a studio.

Queer as Folk (1999)
Set and shot around Greater Manchester.

Clocking Off (2000 to 2002)
Award-winning drama set and filmed in Manchester.

Linda Green (2001 to 2002)
Set and filmed in Manchester.

Phoenix Nights (2001 to 2002)
Peter Kay comedy located and filmed in his home town of Bolton.
The club that features is in the suburb of Farnworth.

Born and Bred (2002 to 2005)
Set in the fictional Lancashire village of Ormston and shot in
the real one of Downham, near Clitheroe.

Cutting It (2002 to 2004)
BBC drama set and filmed in Manchester.

Shameless (2003 onwards)
Filmed for several years on location on a West Gorton estate,
but now shot on a purpose-built set in Wythenshawe.

Blackpool (2004)
Acclaimed musical-drama, filmed in, well, Blackpool.

North and South (2004)
Mill scenes were set in Lancashire mill museums including
Helmshore in Rossendale and Queen Street in Burnley.

Housewife, 49 (2006)
Wartime drama set in Barrow-in-Furness, filmed there and
in Grange-over-Sands.

Life on Mars (2006 to 2007)
Various Lancashire locations have included Manchester
and Bolton.

Longford (2006)
This acclaimed Channel 4 drama about Lord Longford was
filmed at Wymott and Garth Prisons near Leyland.

The Street (2006 onwards)
Set and filmed on a street in Salford.

Waterloo Road (2006 onwards)
Filmed at a school in Rochdale.

19TH-CENTURY LANCASHIRE OCCUPATIONS

One of the wealth of interesting things to be found in the Lancashire
census of 1861 is the list of professions of the time. This top ten shows
the working trends of the age, illustrating in particular Lancashire's
dependence on cotton for employment. Most of the ten professions are
now either rarely found or altogether obsolete.

1   Cotton weaver
2   Servant
3   House keeper
4   Labourer
5   Coal miner
6   Dress maker
7   Cotton winder
8   Cotton spinner
9   Carter
10 Agricultural labourer

HOW TO BUILD A DRY STONE WALL

Gracefully winding their way across fields, hills and dales, dry stone
walls are one of the great wonders of the British countryside. In
Lancashire as in many other rural counties, it is hard to imagine the
landscape without them.

The most recent survey of walls estimated that England has some
70,000 miles (112,655 km) of dry stone walls, with Lancashire home to
at least 10,000 miles (16,095 km). As the name suggests, they are built

without any mortar or cement but are instead held up by the weight of each component stone. That sounds precarious but, properly laid and cared for, a wall can last for centuries, withstanding the worst the weather can throw at it and comfortably outliving rusting fences or cemented walls. They are infinitely preferable to look at too, defining the upland country as surely as the fells or sheep.

Although wall building dates back much further, most of the walls seen today in Lancashire were built in the 18th or 19th centuries to mark the boundaries of common land and protect livestock. Their endurance is testament to the immense skill and labour of the men who built them, and behind every wall of any size lies weeks of backbreaking work, often done in driving rain, howling gales and freezing temperatures.

Although some aspects of wall craft have got easier over the years, the basic techniques have remained the same. Building one is like fitting together a very large, heavy and awkward jigsaw puzzle, in which each and every piece forms an essential part of the whole. Apart from strength and careful assembly, the job involves a large amount of patience, since even the best builder manages no more than a few yards of wall in a day.

A good wall begins with good stone, and builders spend time selecting the best materials - a ton or more of stone for each yard of wall. After that - and the small matter of transporting the stone to an often remote field of hillside - the building starts, and while a few masonry tools and supporting props are used, the job is essentially done by hand. Techniques vary, but most wallers begin by digging out a small trench a few feet wide and a few inches deep, before placing large 'footing' stones snugly inside. Rows of large, flat stones are laid on top, with 'hearting' - smaller chock stones or gravel - tightly filling any gaps that remain in between. For greater strength, walls are often built in double rows parallel to each other, with occasional 'through' stones spanning both to bind them together.

The wall now rises layer by layer, with each stone resting on at least two others below it. Stones must fit together tightly, so that each supports the other and gives the wall strength. For balance, the width tapers as the wall rises, becoming about an inch narrower for each foot it climbs. At the top - usually around 4 or 5 feet high - a row of 'coping' stones is sometimes laid perpendicular or flat, giving the wall a distinctive appearance and making it difficult for animals to clamber over. Some walls also incorporate holes for animals to pass through, or stiles for walkers to climb over.

The art of dry stone walling has undoubtedly declined over the years. With landowners finding it quicker and cheaper to put up fences, some existing walls are starting to decay, and agencies like the National

Trust are campaigning for greater protection and leading some conservation work themselves. But skilled wallers remain in demand, among private garden owners as well as farmers, and Lancashire has a small but busy branch of the Dry Stone Walling Association, running demonstrations and popular training sessions for novices. Its members also compete in dry stone walling competitions, at which they build a stretch of wall from scratch and are judged on its appearance and sturdiness and the speed with which it is prepared. Country shows including Trawden and Great Eccleston also run competitions, and they are good places to understand this wonderful craft and its importance in Lancashire's heritage.

TWENTY ANAGRAMS OF LANCASHIRE

Cleans Hair	Racial Hens	A Clear Shin	Can Heal Sir
Alien Crash	Cars Inhale	Rascal He In	He Cans Liar
Real Chains	Chile Ran As	Char Sale In	Heals In Arc
An Arch Isle	Clash Are In	I Learn Cash	Lean As Rich
Reach Snail	Canal Hires	Clan As Hire	Car Has Line

GREAT LANCASTRIANS –
HENRY TATE

The generations of wealthy merchants and industrialists in 19th-century Lancashire were not, by and large, a philanthropic lot. But there were a handful of businessmen whose concern for the working classes led them to launch lasting social and cultural projects. Sir Henry Tate, the Lancastrian who rose from grocer's boy to multi-millionaire, was among them.

Born in Chorley in 1819, the son of a Unitarian minister, Tate's apprenticeship in Liverpool started at the age of 13. It led him to set up his own grocer's shop at 20, and by 35 he had grown it into a chain of six stores in and around Liverpool. Seeking to expand his interests, he invested in a sugar refining business and took charge of it with his sons when his business partner died in 1869.

'Sugar houses' had existed in Liverpool since the late 17th century. The port provided easy access to sugar cane imported across the Atlantic – much of it carried home by ships sailing the slave routes, though the trade had been abolished by Tate's time – as well as a ready supply of labour. By the mid 19th century the city had a large sugar industry, receiving and refining tens of thousands of tons of cane a year, but Tate advanced it by investing in new techniques – including the patent for sugar cubes – and opening new refineries in Liverpool and London, where he later moved to live. He grew the company into what, after his death and a merger in 1921, became Tate & Lyle, now the largest sugar cane refiner in Europe and a giant multi-national and multi-interest corporation.

Perhaps inspired by his father's values and the deprivation he saw around him in Lancashire, Tate became a generous benefactor as his fortune piled up. He donated to Liverpool's university and hospitals as well as libraries and colleges further afield, often doing so anonymously or discreetly. He did not seek public credit for his projects, and nor did he revolutionise his workers' rights and conditions, but he was said to have expressed genuine concerns for their welfare in private.

Tate's most significant bequest was made in 1889, when he gave his substantial collection of 19th-century British art to the nation, along with £80,000 for the building of a gallery. The resulting building on the site of the old Millbank Prison in London was opened in 1897, although, befitting his modesty, it only became known as the Tate Gallery in the 1930s, well after his death. It became the country's principal repository for contemporary British, and then international, art.

Liverpool has several reminders of Henry Tate's impressive legacy – not least the city's own Tate Gallery, opened in 1988. Liverpool's association with the sugar industry is also explored in the city's excellent museums, including the Merseyside Maritime and International Slavery Museums.

ENGLAND'S LONGEST STANDING SHOP

The Lancashire village of Chipping, halfway between Garstang and Clitheroe in the Forest of Bowland, is home to the oldest shop in the country to have been continuously used as such. Opened in 1668 by a local wool merchant, the shop has housed numerous businesses including a butcher's and an undertaker's. Now, well into its fourth century of trading, it is home to a village store and the Chipping Craft Centre. The pretty village is a conservation area that also has an endowed school dating back to the 17th century and a church that was originally built in the 13th century, though much altered since.

LANCASHIRE'S SEVEN NOBEL LAUREATES

Of the 829 people to have been awarded a Nobel Prize between 1901 and 2009, around 120 were born in Britain or had citizenship there – and seven of them hail from Lancashire. Four have won Nobel's Chemistry Prize, two its Physics and one its Physiology or Medicine; and six of the seven were educated at Manchester or Liverpool universities before going on to study or work elsewhere. In the order they received their honours, Lancashire's seven Nobel laureates are:

J.J. (Joseph John) Thomson (1856–1940; born in Manchester).
Studied in Manchester before conducting most of his research
in Cambridge and London. Awarded the Nobel Prize in Physics
in 1906 following his discovery of the electron.

Charles Barkla (1877–1944; born in Widnes).
Educated at Liverpool University, he received the Prize in
Physics in 1917 for his work on X-ray scattering. He also has
a crater on the moon named in his honour.

Arthur Harden (1865–1940; born in Manchester).
Studied and worked for the first half of his life in his home city,
before receiving the Prize in Chemistry in 1929 for research
into the fermentation of sugar.

Norman Haworth (1883–1950; born in Chorley).
After leaving school at 14 to work in the family business,
Haworth later went against his father's wishes to study
at Manchester University. He received the Prize in Chemistry
in 1937 for his research into vitamins and carbohydrates.

Richard Synge (1914–94; born in Liverpool).
Synge was a renowned biochemist who was awarded the
Prize in Chemistry in 1952 for the invention of partition
chromatography – separating and identifying the components
of a complex mixture.

Rodney Porter (1917–85; born in Newton-le-Willows).
Studied at Liverpool University before moving on to professorships
in London and Cambridge. He received the Prize in Physiology
or Medicine in 1972 for his discovery of the chemical structure
of antibodies.

Michael Smith (1932-2000; born in Blackpool).
Although he was born in Blackpool and received his PhD
at Manchester, Smith did most of his work in Canada. He was
awarded the Prize in Chemistry in 1993 for his research
into mutations in DNA.

LANCASHIRE FOOD – PIES

Few foods stir up as much passion in Lancashire as the humble pie.
Between producers and towns across the county, competition over
who bakes the best is fierce.

Simple to make, cheap and filling, pies have been a staple of
Lancashire eating for centuries, though their modern popularity owes
much to the Industrial Revolution. Baked in advance and conveniently
portable, workers found pies the ideal lunch to take down the mines or
into the mills and factories.

Just as it was then, the classic Lancashire pie is a simple mix of
meat – usually beef – and potato, bound with gravy and topped with
shortcrust pastry. It is commonly served nowadays with chips and
smothered in more gravy or 'pea wet' – the juice from mushy or
marrowfat peas – or, for a carbohydrate-heavy and somewhat messy
meal, wedged in a buttered barm cake or between a couple of slices
of bread. Endless variations on the pie have developed over the years,
though Lancashire loyalists turn their noses up at modern concoctions
like the balti pie.

Small bakers and pie shops were once found all over industrial
Lancashire, though changing public tastes and competition from the
supermarkets mean that many have closed down over the decades.
But the pie remains hugely popular, found on smart pub and restaurant
menus as well as street corner takeaways like fish and chip shops.
Perhaps the best-known brand now is Holland's, which has been baking
in Lancashire for 150 years and is now based at Baxenden near
Accrington, from where it supplies supermarkets across the country
as well as plenty of local outlets.

Lancashire's true centre of pie excellence, however, lies 20 miles
(32 km) further south in Wigan. You don't have to walk far to find
a pie here, and many of their sellers remain small family businesses
rather than the chain bakery companies that dominate other towns'
high streets. Wiganers are often still nicknamed 'pie eaters' – though this
actually refers not to their appetites but to the 1926 General Strike,
when workers were forced by hunger to return to their jobs, so eating

humble pie. In this town and elsewhere, pies remain especially popular among football fans as a half-time snack.

Wigan is also home to the World Pie Eating Championships, an event that is perhaps not quite as prestigious as its title suggests. Health and safety issues mean that the winner is not now the person who eats the most pies in a set time but the person who eats a single pie the quickest, and pressure from vegetarians means that competitors are now offered meat-free alternatives including the traditional butter pie of onions, potatoes, butter and seasonings. Recent contests have encountered controversies, such as when a baker produced pies for the contest that were measured in inches rather than centimetres and thus too big even for Wigan appetites; and when a local dog scoffed the competition's stock the night before the championships.

A recipe for meat and potato pie

500 g braising beef (shin or flank is good)
500 g potatoes
2 medium onions
1 litre beef stock
1 tsp thyme leaves
1 egg
1 pack of shortcrust pastry (or make your own)
2 tbsp plain flour
Salt and freshly ground black pepper
Vegetable oil

Dice the beef into small chunks about an inch (2.5 cm) across, and lightly coat in the flour. Peel and chop the potatoes into similar sized pieces. Peel and roughly chop the onions. Heat a little vegetable oil in a large, thick pan and brown the beef on a high heat, in two batches if necessary. Remove and set aside. Turn the heat on the pan down, add a little more oil and fry the onions. After a few minutes add the potatoes and stir, and a few minutes after that the thyme, stock, salt and pepper. Bring to the boil, cover and simmer gently for about an hour.

Roll out the pastry on a floured table to a thickness of about quarter of an inch (0.5 cm). Pour the meat and potato mixture into a pie dish, leaving out some of the stock if there's too much, and lay the pastry carefully on top. Trim around the edge of the dish, brush all over with the beaten egg, and make a few slits in the top. Bake in a medium oven (200°C / 400°F / gas mark 6) for about forty minutes or until the pastry is golden brown. Serve with mushy peas or pickled red cabbage.

LANCASHIRE'S STEAM RAILWAYS

Of the countless railway lines that were built to serve Lancashire's people and industries in the age of steam, many have fallen out of use. But a small number have been preserved, their tracks and locomotives lovingly brought back to life by the county's dedicated rail buffs. These four lines are all run by railway preservation societies and provide great days out for families in particular.

East Lancashire Railway. Originally opened in 1846 to connect passengers and freight to the Manchester to Bolton line, dwindling use led to it being wound down in the 1970s. A preservation society took on a 12-mile (19 km) stretch from Heywood to Rawtenstall via Bury and Ramsbottom, and ironically passenger numbers are much higher now – around 120,000 a year – than they ever were in its first life. Trains run every weekend and on weekdays in the summer. Tel 0161 764 7790 or visit www.east-lancs-rly.co.uk.

Lakeside and Haverthwaite Railway. In the northernmost chunk of Lancashire, steam engines run along 3.5 miles (5.5 km) of track between the shores of Windermere and Haverthwaite near Newby Bridge. It's the last surviving branch line of the Furness Railway, closed in the 1960s. Services run every day from April to October, as well as over Christmas. Tel 015395 31594 or visit www.lakesiderailway.co.uk.

Ribble Steam Railway. The mile and a half of track on Preston Docks was brought back to life by a group of railway enthusiasts in 2005. It puts to use some of their stock of more than 40 rescued and restored locomotives, previously housed at a museum in Southport but moved here to support the new project. There's a little museum, café and gift shop too; check in advance for train times. Tel 01772 728800 or visit www.ribblesteam.org.uk.

West Lancashire Light Railway. Tiny narrow gauge line around an old clay pit in the village of Hesketh Bank, between Preston and Southport. The quarter of a mile of track has all been laid by the group to run its stock of retired or unwanted locomotives, all painstakingly restored. It carries passengers every Sunday and Bank Holiday Monday from April to October, plus occasional other days. Tel 01772 815881 or visit www.westlancs.org.

Also worth a visit are the Astley Green Colliery Museum near Manchester, which houses some 30 old colliery locomotives and runs demonstrations on a stretch of line though not passenger journeys (visit www.agcm.org.uk); and the Heaton Park Tramway, a nicely restored stretch of the old Manchester Corporation Tramways network (tel 01282 436802 or visit www.heatonparktramway.btik.com).

THE RYDER CUP AND LANCASHIRE

Golf is a thriving sport across Lancashire, but it is a little known fact that the game's most prestigious team trophy – the Ryder Cup – has its origins here.

When the Cup was first contested in 1927, it was a Lancastrian who suggested and supplied it. Samuel Ryder, born in Walton-le-Dale near Preston, made his fortune in business by the unlikely method of selling packets of garden seeds by post at a penny a time – far cheaper than any previous retailer and thus making him very popular among the working classes wishing to tend their plots of land. Starting in the garden shed of his home in his adopted town of St Albans, Hertfordshire, Ryder's headquarters grew into a vast warehouse, with other gardening-related businesses added over the years.

Although cricket was his main sport, Ryder was persuaded to take up golf as a way to relieve the stresses of business and improve his often poor health, and he soon became hooked on it. After sponsoring several tournaments, he contributed a trophy for an exhibition international match in 1926, and later suggested that it should become a regular event for the best professional golfers of the US and Britain (and, later, Europe). He paid for a gold trophy to be made at a cost of £250 – a bargain by modern sponsorship standards, though the event in its early years was intended simply as a friendly, social occasion for its participants. The figure preparing to swing his club on the top of the trophy is Abe Mitchell, a popular golfer of his day and, more to the point, Ryder's private tutor.

Starting in the US, the tournament has been played every two years since on alternate sides of the Atlantic, except during the Second World War. Ryder saw Britain win his cup on home soil twice before his death in 1936, and, fittingly, it has been contested in Lancashire six times: at the Southport and Ainsdale club in 1933 and 1937; the Royal Lytham and St Annes club in 1961 and 1977; and the Royal Birkdale club in Southport in 1965 and 1969.

LANCASHIRE FARMING

As it has all over the country, farming in Lancashire has been beset by difficulties lately – the pressure on prices and the foot and mouth crisis of 2001 among them. The industry has declined dramatically, and the number of people working on farms in Lancashire is around a third lower than it was even a few decades ago. But it nevertheless remains a significant contributor to the county's economy, and the diversification of many farms – into accommodation, farm shops, farmers' markets and the like – has helped them to get through the succession of challenges.

These statistics about farming in the region are compiled by the Department for Environment, Food and Rural Affairs (DEFRA). Statistics for the various modern-day administrative regions of the county have been combined to give figures for an approximation of Lancashire as defined by its historic boundaries.

9,670 . . . . . . total farm holdings (a holding is defined as land farmed in one unit, and farms can have more than one holding)

2,424 . . . . holdings that are used for grazing lifestock

794 . . . . dairy farm holdings

313 . . . . cereal farm holdings

4,505 . . . . farm holdings that are under 12 acres (5 ha) in size

675 . . . . farm holdings that are more than 247 acres (100 ha) in size

1,108 . . . . total square miles (2,870 sq km) of farmed land

4,862 . . . . full-time farmers and spouses

16,228 . . . . total farm labour

3,471,430 . . . . chickens held on farms

774,556 . . . . sheep

259,440 . . . . cattle

74,128 . . . . pigs

27,041 . . . . ducks

17,528 . . . . turkeys

15,691 . . . . horses

5,899 . . . . geese

2,339 . . . . goats

HOW TO WORK OUT THE WIND CHILL

Even the hardiest of Lancastrians would be hard-pushed to deny that it can get a bit chilly in the county at times. And when the wind whips over Lancashire's exposed fells and moors, the temperature can seem a good deal lower than the weather forecast promised. This is the wind chill – the temperature that is felt on exposed skin rather than the air measurement. Lots of different methods have been used to measure and index wind chill, but the snappy formula currently used by the Met Office is as follows:

Wind Chill = 35.74 + 0.6215T – 35.75(V$^{0.16}$)+ 0.4275(V$^{0.16}$)
Where T is the air temperature in ° Fahrenheit and V is the wind speed in miles per hour.

This table shows the wind chill according to the air temperature and wind. With an air temperature of 30°F (-1°C) and wind of 40 mph (64 kph) for instance, the wind chill is 13°F (-10°C). Frostbite can set in in less than 30 minutes if the wind chill falls beneath -18°F (-28°C). So wrap up warm.

Wind in mph (kmp)

Air temp °F (°C)	10 (16)	20 (32)	30 (48)	40 (64)	50 (80)	60 (96)
50 (10)	46 (8)	44 (7)	42 (6)	41 (5)	40 (4.5)	39 (4)
40 (4)	34 (1)	30 (-1)	28 (-2)	27 (-3)	26(-3.5)	25 (-4)
30 (-1)	21 (-6)	17 (-8)	15 (-9)	13 (-10)	12 (-11)	10 (-12)
20 (-7)	9 (-13)	4 (-16)	1 (-17)	-1 (-18)	-3 (-19)	-4 (-20)

LANCASHIRE'S FOOTBALL HONOURS BOARD

Football clubs from Lancashire have won the top tier of England's football league – the old Division One and now the Premier League – no fewer than 54 times since it was first contested in 1888. On average, therefore, a Lancashire club has taken the honour nearly every other year. Leading the list by some distance are the area's two footballing giants, Liverpool and Manchester United, with 18 titles apiece. Everton have nine, and the only other Lancashire club to have won the league since the 1960s is Blackburn Rovers, who have three titles in all. Burnley, Manchester City and Preston North End have two each.

England's other leading football competition, the FA Cup, has gone to Lancashire 44 times since it was first organised in 1872. Manchester United and Liverpool again lead this roll call, and each of Lancashire's league winners have won this competition too. Other clubs to have claimed the trophy are Bolton Wanderers, Bury, Blackpool and the long defunct Blackburn Olympic. Liverpool and Manchester United have also won Europe's leading competition – the European Cup and now the Champions League – eight times between them.

That tally of more than one hundred major titles makes Lancashire the centre of footballing excellence in England. Clubs from London and Yorkshire, by comparison, have won the football league just 18 and 11 times respectively.

League champions

18 Liverpool (1901, 1906, 1922, 1923, 1947, 1964, 1966, 1973, 1976, 1977, 1979, 1980, 1982, 1983, 1984, 1986, 1988, 1990)

18 Manchester United (1908, 1911, 1952, 1956, 1957, 1965, 1967, 1993, 1994, 1996, 1997, 1999, 2000, 2001, 2003, 2007, 2008, 2009)

9 Everton (1891, 1915, 1928, 1932, 1939, 1963, 1970, 1985, 1987)

3 Blackburn Rovers (1912, 1914, 1995)

2 Burnley (1921, 1960)

2 Manchester City (1937, 1968)

2 Preston North End (1889, 1890)

FA Cup winners

11 Manchester United (1909, 1948, 1963, 1977, 1983, 1985, 1990, 1994, 1996, 1999, 2004)

7 Liverpool (1965, 1974, 1986, 1989, 1992, 2001, 2006)

6 Blackburn Rovers (1884, 1885, 1886, 1890, 1891, 1928)

5 Everton (1906, 1933, 1966, 1984, 1995)

4 Bolton Wanderers (1923, 1926, 1929, 1958)

4 Manchester City (1904, 1934, 1956, 1969)

2 Bury (1900, 1903)

2 Preston North End (1889, 1938)

1 Blackburn Olympic (1883)

1 Blackpool (1953)

1 Burnley (1914)

European Cup winners

5 Liverpool (1977, 1978, 1981, 1984, 2005)

3 Manchester United (1968, 1999, 2008)

LANCASHIRE'S GREATEST WALKER

The Lake District has been home and inspiration to dozens of famous poets and novelists down the centuries, but no modern writer is so widely read or revered as Lancashire's own Alfred Wainwright. Few have walked as extensively across the Lakes as he, and no-one has chronicled the area's glorious fells, a good number of which are within the county's original boundaries, half so well.

Wainwright was born in Blackburn in 1907, and the contrast between the town's bleak industrial landscape and the peaceful emptiness of the Lake District was immediately apparent on his first holiday there at the age of 23. 'I was utterly enslaved by all I saw,' he wrote later. 'Here were no huge factories, but mountains; no stagnant canals, but sparking crystal-clear rivers; no cinder paths but beckoning tracks that clamber through bracken and heather to the silent fastnesses of the hills. That week changed my life.'

Wainwright settled in Kendal in his thirties, but it wasn't until the early 1950s that he had the idea of producing pen and ink drawings of the mountains he climbed, together with detailed records of the routes to their tops and the views once there. Having divided what he considered the Lake District's 214 'true' fells over 1,000 feet (305 m) in height into seven regions, he set himself a 13-year schedule to climb and write about them all. The project was initially done for pleasure, with little idea of writing a book, but having compiled his first set of notes he approached a printer to produce copies of the first of his *Pictorial Guides to the Lakeland Fells*. The book was immediately popular, and thousands of walkers eagerly anticipated his next installments until the seventh and final volume was published in 1965.

Wainwright's books were, by his own admission, a labour of love. Having walked all weekend, Wainwright would write up his notes from the fells at home through the following week, adding sketches based on photographs he had taken. Each book was entirely handwritten page by page, immaculately formatted and presented ready for the printer's press. If he made a mistake on a page, he tore it up and started again. Astonishingly, Wainwright completed all his travels to and from his walks on public transport and without the aid of a car – and all seven *Pictorial Guides* were written while he held down a full-time job as borough treasurer at Kendal.

Wainwright went on to produce many more books about the peripheries of the Lake District and other areas, as well as various collections of drawings and memoirs. He participated rather reluctantly in a TV series, and created the Coast to Coast walk from St Bees in

Cumbria to Robin Hood's Bay in Yorkshire, now one of the most popular long-distance trails in Britain. But although a small fortune of royalties poured in, he never wrote any of his books for money, instead donating a large proportion of it to Cumbrian animal charities.

Several decades after they were first published, Wainwright's books remain hugely popular, and have recently been thoroughly updated for another generation of walkers. Because so many hikers by nature relish a good challenge and a list of peaks to bag, emulating Wainwright's feat has become a popular obsession – a challenge sometimes taken on over a year or even a summer, but more usually over a lifetime. Athletes have battled to complete the summits the quickest – the record of six days and 23 hours was set by legendary fell runner Joss Naylor – while other remarkable rounds have included that of Robin Regan, who had notched up all 214 peaks by the age of just five.

Wainwright is remembered in his home town by a blue plaque on the house in which he grew up, though a more substantial commemoration is to be found at St James' Church in Buttermere in the northern Lake District, within sight of Haystacks, his favourite fell and the one on which his ashes were scattered after his death in 1991. Blackburn's Thwaites brewery has an ale named in his honour, while the Wainwright Society was formed in 2002 to celebrate his work and values. The greatest memorials of all, though, are Wainwright's exquisite and timeless books that he called his 'love letters' to the Lakes.

LANCASHIRE'S PIERS

For coastal holidaymakers in Lancashire, the pier is an essential part of the seaside experience. Of the 55 piers that the National Piers Society records as surviving in the UK, Lancashire has five, all opened within a few decades of one another in the late 19th century. In descending order of length and with their year of opening, they are:

Southport (3,635 feet / 1,108 metres; opened in 1860)
Blackpool North (1,319 feet / 402 metres; opened in 1863)
Blackpool Central (1,119 feet / 341 metres; opened in 1868)
St Annes (600 feet / 183 metres; opened in 1885)
Blackpool South (492 feet / 150 metres; opened in 1893)

As well as being Lancashire's longest, Southport is also the UK's second longest pier after Southend, which extends 7,201 feet (2,195 m). Lancashire has four more piers that are now either closed to the public or destroyed altogether: Lytham (closed in 1960), Morecambe West End (1978), Morecambe Central (1992) and Fleetwood (2008).

ENTERTAINERS FROM LANCASHIRE

Perhaps because of its tradition of seaside entertainment, Lancashire has produced a steady stream of comedians, TV and radio personalities and other entertainers over the years. Here are 30 of the best known, with the place of their birth in brackets.

Zoe Ball (Blackpool)
Cilla Black (Liverpool)
Jim Bowen (Accrington)
Tommy Cannon and Bobby Ball (Oldham)
Judith Chalmers (Manchester)
Steve Coogan (Manchester)
Alistair Cooke (Manchester)
John Culshaw (Ormskirk)
Les Dawson (Manchester)
Fred Dibnah (Bolton)
David Dickinson (Manchester)
Ken Dodd (Liverpool)
Chris Evans (Warrington)
Judy Finnegan (Manchester)
Kerry Katona (Warrington)
Peter Kay (Bolton)
Vernon Kay (Bolton)
Matthew Kelly (Urmston)
Stan Laurel (Ulverston)
Lee Mack (Blackburn)
Bernard Manning (Manchester)
Eric Morecambe (Morecambe)
Bill Oddie (Rochdale)
Nick Park (Walner Bridge)
Anne Robinson (Crosby)
Philip Schofield (Oldham)
Dave Spikey (Farnworth)
Eric Sykes (Oldham)
Johnny Vegas (St Helens)
Victoria Wood (Prestwich)

SOBERING UP

Given the wealth of pubs and breweries in Lancashire these days it is hard to believe that this was, for a while at least, one of the most sober parts of the country.

As cheap alcohol and alcoholism spread across the industrialising towns of the north, Lancashire was one of the first places to react against it. It was in Preston in the 1830s that Britain's Temperance Movement began, first encouraging moderation in drinking and then soon total abstinence. The movement gradually spread across the densely populated towns of the county, where alcoholism frequently wrecked family life. Temperance was enthusiastically encouraged by both the church – especially Methodists – and mill owners, for whom drunkenness reduced productivity.

To keep people happy as well as sober, and to prove that they could have a good time without recourse to the demon drink, temperance bars began to spring up across Lancashire. Many grew out of herbalist shops and would serve increasingly imaginative soft drinks like ginger beer, dandelion and burdock and sarsaparilla. One of the most popular bars was Fitzpatrick's, a chain set up by an Irish family of herbalists that at its peak had more than 20 outlets. Those drinking in the bars would often be asked to take a Temperance Pledge, like this one for Fitzpatrick's:

> A pledge we make, no wine to take,
> No brandy red that turns the head,
> Nor fiery rum that ruins home,
> Nor whiskey hot that turns the sot,
> Nor brewers beer, for that we fear,
> Feel instead Fitzpatrick's cheer!

Despite their noble intentions, the lure of Lancashire's alcoholic drinks was obviously too strong. Rising leisure time and incomes, the end of prohibition in the US, the introduction of free medicine and a more balanced attitude towards alcohol all sped the decline, and the bars across Lancashire gradually closed. The last remaining one is Fitzpatrick's branch on Bank Street in Rawtenstall, which trades as much on its nostalgic appeal as it does on the range of non-alcoholic drinks it still produces and sells, including cordials, herbal tonics and the original recipe sarsaparilla.

LANCASHIRE ON SCREEN –
BRIEF ENCOUNTER

Few British movies evoke such passionate nostalgia as *Brief Encounter*, and few filming locations attract as many fans as Carnforth Station in northern Lancashire.

When shooting for the film was scheduled in the last months of the Second World War in 1945, the film's producers initially wanted to use a London station. But realising that blackout regulations and the lingering threat of air raids would make night-time filming impossible, they sought alternatives. Carnforth fitted the bill, partly because it had slopes rather than stairs connecting the platforms – much easier for actors Celia Johnson and Trevor Howard, as well as film crews, to navigate.

At the time of filming Carnforth was a busy junction on the London, Midland and Scottish Railway, providing plenty of opportunities for crowd and train scenes as well as a ready supply of local extras. In the decades after the war, though, the decline of steam, falling passenger numbers and the reorganisation of rail lines all led to the station becoming neglected, and at several times its future was threatened. *Brief Encounter* may just have saved it, and its film connections certainly provided a strong argument for a much-needed refurbishment in 2000. Many of the period features on the station were tidied up, and the clock featured in the film rediscovered and reinstalled above the platforms.

Although only around a fifth of *Brief Encounter* was actually shot on location at Carnforth, the station provides many of its most memorable moments, and aside from a few modern additions, the platforms themselves are much as Johnson and Howard found them in 1945. The most famous scenes of all are those staged in the station's refreshment room, though these were actually shot in a recreated set in a southern film studio. This set, however, was closely based on Carnforth's actual refreshment room, which has also been very carefully restored to how it looks in the film. It now serves tea and cake to coach loads of dewy-eyed film fans.

The refurbishment also gave the station an excellent visitors' centre, featuring photos and memorabilia from the filming of *Brief Encounter* as well as exhibitions on other interesting aspects of its history. The film plays on a loop here, providing a constant reminder of the station's role in film history. These days it serves only a branch line from Lancashire into Cumbria, but more than 60 years on, the popularity of the film is such that it now gets as many people wanting to linger on its platforms and in its rooms as it does train passengers.

THE ULTIMATE CRICKET TEAM?

Followers of Lancashire's county cricket team have spent countless hours arguing about their club's best ever players. This eleven is based purely on statistics rather than opinions about the relative skills of players, and features Lancashire's six highest first-class run scorers, the four highest wicket takers and the most prolific wicket-keeper. As such, the line-up is heavily biased towards the eras around the two world wars, when cricketers played many more matches than they do now, and were able to set career totals for runs and wickets that modern-day players can never hope to surpass. The only two to have played any of their cricket after 1950 are batsman Cyril Washbrook and bowler Brian Statham. Four of the eleven began their careers in the 19th century.

Lancashire's fantasy team features two brothers, Ernest and John Tyldesley, who between them scored more than 66,000 runs for Lancashire, and a third but unrelated Tyldesley, bowler Dick. Other notable players include batsman Harry Makepeace, one of only a handful of men to have played both cricket and football for England; Johnny Briggs, a canny slow bowler who developed a mental illness and died at just 39; and Arthur Mold, a much feared fast bowler whose career was ended when his action was judged unlawful.

1   Ernest Tyldesley (34,222 runs)
2   John Tyldesley (31,949 runs)
3   Cyril Washbrook (27,863 runs)
4   Harry Makepeace (25,207 runs)
5   Frank Watson (22,833 runs)
6   Jack Sharp (22,015 runs)
7   George Duckworth (635 catches and 290 stumpings)
8   Brian Statham (1,816 wickets)
9   Johnny Briggs (1,696 wickets)
10   Arthur Mold (1,541 wickets)
11   Dick Tyldesley (1,449 wickets)

TEN ANIMAL ATTRACTIONS

A selection of Lancashire's best animal attractions offering days out for young and old.

Blackpool Zoo.
On the site of what was once Blackpool Airport, this is one
of the biggest zoos in the northwest with around 1,500 animals.
Tel 01253 830830 or visit www.blackpoolzoo.org.uk.

Bowland Wild Boar Park, Chipping.
Family-friendly park in the Forest of Bowland, with deer,
llamas and red squirrels as well as packs of wild boar.
Tel 01995 61554 or visit www.wildboarpark.co.uk.

The Butterfly House, Lancaster.
Large collection of exotic butterflies in the old palm house at the
city's Williamson Park, which also has animal and bird enclosures.
Tel 01524 33318 or visit www.williamsonpark.com.

Easterleigh Animal Sanctuary, St Annes.
Large sanctuary housing hundreds of different animals.
Tel 01253 789185 or visit www.easterleigh.org.uk.

Leighton Moss, near Carnforth.
The largest reedbed in the northwest, home to dozens of
unusual birds and with trails and hides for spotters.
Tel 01524 701601 or visit www.rspb.org.uk/leightonmoss.

Martin Mere, near Ormskirk.
A large wetland habitat, home to more than a hundred species of
mammals and birds including some rare and migratory species.
Tel 01704 895181 or visit www.wwt.org.uk/martinmere.

Old Holly Farm, near Garstang.
One of a new breed of working farms that have opened up to
the public. This one is organic and puts the emphasis on feeding
and stroking the animals.
Tel 01524 791200 or visit wwww.oldhollyfarm.com.

Penny Farm, near Blackpool.
A World Horse Welfare centre that rescues and rehabilitates
around 60 horses a year and welcomes visitors at weekends.
Tel 01253 766983 or visit www.worldhorsewelfare.org.

Sea Life, Blackpool.
One of the country's biggest aquariums with more than a
thousand different creatures including tropical sharks.
Tel 0871 423 2110 or visit www.sealifeeurope.com/blackpool.

Turbary Woods Owl and Bird of Prey Sanctuary, Whitestake.
Woodland sanctuary and rehabilitation centre with around a
hundred birds including eagles, hawks, falcons, buzzards and vultures.
Tel 01772 323323 or visit www.turbarywoods.co.uk.

PENDLE HILL, WITCHES AND QUAKERS

On the face of it, Pendle Hill is a rather unassuming peak – a lonely
plateau a few miles east of Clitheroe that reaches a height of 1,828 feet
(557 m). But a few remarkable events there in the 17th century mean
that it is now perhaps the most famous and climbed hill in Lancashire.

In 1612, the area around Pendle was the focal point of one of the
most famous witch-hunts in British history, when eleven women and
men were first pursued by suspicious locals and magistrates and then
put on trial. Quite why the area harboured so many suspected witches
is unclear, but it had certainly developed something of a reputation
for religious dissent and unruly behaviour. The accused were probably
p ractising their idea of witch c raft – perhaps 'treating' people with spells
as a way of making money, but they came to be blamed for several
illnesses and deaths as well as sundry other crimes. After cursory trials
at Lancaster Assizes – now Lancaster Castle – nine of the accused were
hanged on a hill above the town.

The air of superstition and religious persecution meant Pendle's
was far from the only witch trial of the time, and up to 500 'witches'
are thought to have been executed in England between the 15th and
18th centuries. But thanks to some assiduous note-taking by the clerk
of Lancaster's court, this is one of the events for which the most
documented evidence has been found.

A more uplifting aspect of Pendle's history is its association with the
Quaker movement. It was on top of the hill, 40 years later in 1652, that
the movement's founder, George Fox, claimed to have experienced a
vision that became significant in his development of the movement
that became known as the Religious Society of Friends. Fox wrote in his
memoirs: 'As we travelled we came near a very great hill, called Pendle
Hill, and I was moved of the Lord to go up to the top of it – which I did
with difficulty, it was so very steep and high. When I was come to the
top, I saw the sea bordering upon Lancashire. From the top of this hill
the Lord let me see in what places he had a great people to be gathere d.'

Pendle Hill's history means it continues to be popular with both
those interested in witchcraft and Quakers following in Fox's footsteps.
Its slopes are especially busy every Halloween, and ghost hunters claim

it is one of the most haunted places in the country. The local council has a 45-mile (72 km) 'Witches Trail', leading from Pendle Hill through the Ribble Valley to Lancaster, while a Burnley brewery, Moorhouses, offers a popular 'Witches Brew' beer. The hill's name also lends itself to a major Quaker centre in the US state of Pennsylvania, founded by prominent Quaker William Penn.

In an area of the country that reputedly gets more than its fair share of damp days, the hill is also renowned as a weather predictor. 'If you can see Pendle then it's about to rain,' goes a local saying, 'And if you can't then it's already started.'

A BEATLES TRAIL OF LIVERPOOL

Liverpool's many connections to The Beatles help it to attract thousands of music fans each year. Here are ten places in the city that were significant in the history of the band and where Beatles aficionados can find out more about John, Paul, George and Ringo.

20 Forthlin Road. Paul McCartney grew up in this 1920s
terraced house, and the Beatles wrote and rehearsed
their early songs here. It is now owned by the National Trust
and restored to its 1960s appearance.
Visits are by guided tour only.

Mendips. John Lennon's childhood home on Menlove
Avenue, also now owned by the National Trust and
evocatively restored to its 1960s state, and only accessible
by pre-booked tour (tel 0844 800 4791 or visit
www.nationaltrust.org.uk/beatles).

Liverpool Institute for Performing Arts. This was
once the Liverpool Institute High School for Boys, the
grammar school attended by McCartney and George Harrison
from 1953. It was closed in 1985 but with McCartney's help
reopened as an arts and entertainment training centre
11 years later.

St Peter's Church Hall. This unassuming little hall in
Woolton secured its place in music history when John
Lennon and Paul McCartney met at a fete here in 1957.
The church's graveyard has the gravestone of Eleanor Rigby.

Casbah Coffee Club. This basement club in the West Derby suburb, run by Pete Best's mother, is where The Beatles talked and played in their early days. It is open to the public, but only on pre-booked tours (tel 0151 280 3519).

Cavern Club. A cellar club on Mathew Street at which The Beatles played nearly 300 times. It is also where manager Brian Epstein first spotted the band. Now largely rebuilt, it is open to the public every day and hosts music acts most nights, including Beatles tribute bands (tel 0151 236 1965 or visit www.cavernclub.org).

38 Kensington. This small terraced house was once Percy Phillips' studio, where Beatles members made their first ever recording as The Quarrymen in 1958. A blue plaque now marks its importance.

Penny Lane. The street that inspired the 1967 song is in the Mossley Hill part of the city, near where Lennon and McCartney grew up, and is named after James Penny, an 18th-century slave trader. Street signs here are among the most frequently photographed and stolen in the UK.

Strawberry Field. 'Strawberry Fields Forever', the flip side to the 'Penny Lane' single, was inspired by Strawberry Field, an estate in Woolton. Owned by the Salvation Army it was a children's home until 2007, and the heavily-graffitied gates and wall remain.

The Beatles Story. The city's major attraction for fans making a pilgrimage, it tells an exhaustive story of the band and has some fun interactive elements. It's at Albert Dock and opens every day bar Christmas (tel 0151 709 1963 or visit www.beatlesstory.com).

LANCASHIRE'S BIGGEST PUDDING

Most Lancastrians have healthy appetites, but the biggest of all must belong to the residents of Aughton, a village near the River Lune in the north of the county. Here, in the early 18th century, villagers produced a giant plum pudding as part of celebrations to mark the cropping of local willow that was used by local weavers. The custom was repeated every 21 years until 1886, when a pudding was made weighing 560 kg and incorporating 50 kg of flour, 70 kg of sugar, 135 kg of dried fruit and 900 eggs. Perhaps sensing that it would be difficult to top that, Aughton's tradition was then suspended for the best part of a century, but revived in the 1970s.

LANCASHIRE'S UNIVERSITIES

Measured by its traditional rather than modern-day administrative boundaries, Lancashire has ten universities. They are:

University of Bolton
University of Central Lancashire
Edge Hill University (Ormskirk)
Lancaster University
University of Liverpool
Liverpool Hope University
Liverpool John Moores University
University of Manchester
Manchester Metropolitan University
University of Salford

Lancashire is also home to campuses of the University of Cumbria in Lancaster and the University of Huddersfield in Oldham.

THE DUCHY OF LANCASTER

Whether you consider it a valuable connection to the country's royal history or an unjustifiable anachronism, the Duchy of Lancaster is a significant part of Lancashire's history.

Along with a counterpart in Cornwall, Lancaster is one of the two surviving royal duchies in England. It was created in 1265, when King Henry III granted land to his son, Edmund. Nearly a century later Edmund's grandson became the first Duke of Lancaster, and he took control of the newly created Lancashire when it was designated as a county palatine with powers independent of the monarch. Then, as now, the Duchy took in territory across the country, and not just in Lancashire. Early acquisitions included estates in London, Leicestershire, Northamptonshire and Staffordshire, and they have been added to over the centuries. Since 1399 the title of Duke of Lancaster has been assumed by the reigning monarch, and the Duchy has been considered his or her personal property rather than part of the Crown Estate.

The current Duchy covers some 46,456 acres (18,800 ha) or 73 square miles (189 sq km) of land in England and Wales, and takes in urban developments, farm land and businesses as well as more traditional estates and historic buildings. Its properties within Lancashire include Lancaster Castle - nowadays leased to the county council - while its appointments include the official Morecambe Bay Guides, whose job it is to lead walkers across the dangerous sands of the Bay. Further afield, it owns or leases Halton, Peveril, Bolingbroke, Tutbury and Knaresborough Castles in Cheshire, Derbyshire, Lincolnshire, Staffordshire and Yorkshire respectively, as well as the Savoy Chapel in London. The portfolio is split into four Rural Surveys - the Lancashire, Yorkshire, Needwood and Crewe and South Surveys - plus one Urban Survey.

The Duchy now operates as a thoroughly modern property management business, providing a substantial income for the Queen that is intended to subsidise the costs of her official commitments. In 2009, its possessions were valued at £323 million, and it returns an annual operating profit of £10 million to £15 million. Many of the traditions of the Duchy have now died out, though some, like the appointment of High Sheriffs for the modern counties of Lancashire, Greater Manchester and Merseyside, continue. The appointment is now largely ceremonial, and is officially made by the Queen by the distinctly archaic method of marking parchments with a bodkin. Another reminder of the Duchy comes in Lancashire's form of the loyal toast, which is made 'to the Queen, Duke of Lancaster'.

LANCASHIRE'S CANALS

Lancashire's canals are now largely sedate, making it hard to imagine that they ever formed a bustling network. But in their heyday in the late 18th and early 19th centuries, inland waterways were vital to the burgeoning industries of the northwest, and linked Lancashire with the rest of the world. Their barges transported coal, limestone, cotton and other important imports and exports along an infrastructure that was itself a massive feat of engineering.

Railways, roads and the decline of industry led to many of Lancashire's canals falling into disrepair in the 20th century, but they are now a focus of regeneration – their waters and towpaths popular with leisure boaters, walkers and cyclists along their rural stretches, and thronged with retail and café developments beside their urban ones. These are Lancashire's eleven canals.

Bridgewater Canal. Opened in 1761, this is often considered England's first 'proper' canal, and it inspired the building of many more soon afterwards. It took coal from mines at Worsley to Manchester and was soon extended on to Runcorn, with connections to several other canals along the way. It remains one of the few privately owned canals in the country, and is popular for cruising.

Sankey Canal. Built to transport coal from Lancashire's coalfields up to Liverpool, it ran 15 miles (24 km) from St Helens to the River Mersey at Widnes and rivals the Bridgewater for the title of the country's first canal of the Industrial Revolution. It closed in the 1960s, but a restoration society is leading efforts to make it fully navigable again.

Rochdale Canal. Continues on from the Bridgewater Canal to cross the Pennines to Sowerby Bridge in Yorkshire. Opened in 1804, it became the major route for commerce between the red and white rose counties, carrying up to 50 barges a day. Declining use meant the canal fell into disrepair in the 20th century, but it has now been fully restored for boating. Its hilly route means there are 92 locks along its 32 miles (51 km) – but great views too.

Leeds and Liverpool Canal. At 127 miles (204 km), this is the longest canal to have been built as a single waterway in Britain, and the second longest of all behind the Grand Union. Built to service cross-Pennine trade and industry, work started in 1770 but the canal took nearly 50 years to complete. With river connections from Leeds out to the sea, it offers a way from coast to coast without ever touching land.

Lancaster Canal. Originally intended to run from Westhoughton near Bolton up to Kendal in the southern Lake District, only the 40-mile (64 km) stretch from Preston to near Carnforth is now navigable, though there are plans to extend it northwards. It's a contour canal, built to follow the lie of the land and so requiring no locks. Cruises run up and down the scenic canal, taking in the spectacular Lune Aqueduct.

Ashton Canal. A short canal that runs from the Rochdale Canal in Manchester out to the Huddersfield Canal at Ashton-under-Lyne near

Lancashire's Yorkshire border. It opened around 1800 and initially flourished, but use declined over the years and it was effectively closed in the 1960s. Repairs then made it fully navigable again.

Manchester, Bolton and Bury Canal. Opened in 1796 and ran from Salford to Prestolee, where it forked to the two important industrial towns of Bolton and Bury. Declining use and a breach in 1936 caused it to be closed, but a major refurbishment is now underway.

Manchester Ship Canal. A monumental feat of Victorian engineering, this was the world's biggest navigational canal when it opened in the late 19th century. It was built to connect Manchester to the sea, and turned it for a while into one of Britain's busiest ports, despite being some 40 miles (64 km) inland. Known locally as the Big Ditch, it remains an important cargo route, carrying around 6 million tons of freight a year.

Huddersfield Narrow Canal. Another trans-Pennine canal, it runs from Huddersfield in Yorkshire to the fringes of Lancashire at Ashton-under-Lyne.

Peak Forest Canal. A narrow, 15-mile (24 km) canal that runs out of Lancashire from Ashton-under-Lyne to Bugsworth in Derbyshire. It was built to bring limestone from the quarries up to Manchester.

Ribble Link. When it was opened in 2002, this was the first canal ever to be built in Britain for leisure use, and the first of any kind in nearly a century. It connects the Lancaster Canal to the River Ribble over a 4-mile (6 km) stretch around Preston, along which boats must book their passage in advance.

GREAT LANCASTRIANS – RICHARD ARKWRIGHT

Lancashire's success in the textile industry can mostly be attributed to the labour and skill of its thousands of workers. But more than any other individual, Richard Arkwright can be credited with establishing the county as a cotton powerhouse and, what's more, the home of mass, powered production.

Arkwright was born in Preston in 1732, the youngest of 13 children in a poor family, and was taught to read and write by his cousin.

After starting work as a barber's apprentice, he made his first forays as an entrepreneur in his twenties by setting up as a wig manufacturer and hair dyer. He had taken an interest in the textile industry on business trips around Lancashire towns, and met John Kay, a Warrington dockmaker who had been wo rking on ways to mechanise the processes of weaving. With Arkwright investing funds and Kay refining the details, the pair produced a new frame that built on the spinning jenny introduced by James Hargreaves, a Lancashire weaver and inventor, and became known as the water frame.

Before Hargreaves, Arkwright and Kay, producing cloth was a slow, fiddly and laborious process. With the new machinery, however, it was a much more efficient process, the new frame able to spin multiple threads fast and continuously with high quality results. Arkwright quickly realised that mass production of textiles was now possible, and in 1771 he opened the world's first water-powered mill in Cromford, Derbyshire. Others soon followed, in Staffordshire and Scotland as well as Derbyshire and back in his home county, and Arkwright soon had thousands of workers toiling in an empire of mills. The factory system that he created was as tough as most images of Lancashire's cotton mills suggest, employing children and women as well as men on 13-hour shifts in uncomfortable and often dangerous conditions. Arkwright also pioneered the factory village, a complex of houses and facilities for his workers – though this was inspired less by philanthropic concern than a desire to keep them close at hand and in his debt.

All this makes Arkwright the father of at least Lancashire's new textile industry, if not much of the wider Industrial Revolution. It also made him exceptionally wealthy, and when he died in 1792, he left a fortune of around half a million pounds – worth perhaps a hundred times that amount in today's money. But he also made plenty of enemies – not least the hand weavers of Lancashire whom he first put out of jobs with the industrialisation of their work, and then virtually enslaved in his factories when they could find no other employment. Many of the inventors he worked with later became angry at what they regarded as intellectual theft, and other manufacturers faced down attempts made by Arkwright to put them out of business by claiming patents on his machinery. Arkwright was no great inventor or thinker, but like few others in Lancashire before or since, he knew how to make ideas and labour pay.

The Harris Museum in Arkwright's home town of Preston has material about him and a model of the revolutionary water frame (tel 01772 258248 or visit www.harrismuseum.org.uk). There is more about Arkwright and the cotton industry at the Helmshore Mills Textile Museum in Rossendale (tel 01706 226459 or visit www.lancashire.gov.uk). Cromford Mill is being restored by the Arkwright Society and is now a World Heritage Site in recognition of its importance to the Industrial Revolution.

LANCASHIRE'S OLDEST BUSINESSES

Lancashire has a rich history of successful small and independent businesses, and boasts more than 150 firms that can trace their histories back more than a century. This list of the 20 longest established firms in the county is headed by a Preston and Lancaster-based solicitors' practice, Blackhurst, Swainson, Goodier, that has been providing legal services continuously for nearly three centuries. Six more solicitors also feature on the list, along with a host of small shops, service providers and engineering or building related companies.

Business	Activity	Location	Founded
Blackhurst, Swainson, Goodier	Solicitors	Preston/Lancaster	1720
Henry Ibbotson & Son	Builders	Blackburn	1756
Woodcock & Sons	Solicitors	Various	1791
Southerns	Solicitors	Various	1792
Dickson Haslam	Solicitors	Various	1797
James Baxter & Son	Potted shrimps	Morecambe	1799
Napthens	Solicitors	Various	1800
James Thornber	Textiles	Clitheroe	1800*
Mears Flooring	Carpets etc.	Preston	1802
Daniel Thwaites	Brewery	Blackburn	1807
Oglethorpe Sturton & Gillibrand	Solicitors	Lancaster	1810
Dickinson Parker Hill	Solicitors	Ormskirk	1810*
R.K. Timber	Timber products	Chorley	1814
S. Carr & Son	Jewellers	Garstang	1820
Askam Construction	Civil engineering	Lancaster	1831
E.T. Birtwistle & Sons	Funeral directors	Blackburn	1832
Platt's of Preston	Pen shop	Preston	1832
BCH (now Coates Engineering)	Food science	Whitworth	1835
J. Atkinson & Co.	Tea and coffee	Lancaster	1837
Lawsons	Luggage etc.	Lancaster	1837

* Estimated rather than documented

⟨C⟩⟨C⟩⟨C⟩⟨C⟩⟨C⟩⟨C⟩⟨C⟩⟨C⟩⟨C⟩⟨C⟩⟨C⟩⟨C⟩⟨C⟩⟨C⟩⟨C⟩⟨C⟩⟨C⟩⟨C⟩

LANCASTRIANS IN THE RUGBY LEAGUE HALL OF FAME

Of the 17 players to have been inducted into English rugby league's official hall of fame, three were born in Lancashire. Together with Yorkshire, the county is the English capital of rugby league, and all three players we re either born in or played for St Helens, the Merseyside town that has long been a powerhouse of the sport. Eligibility for the hall of fame is restricted to those who played the sport in England for at least ten years, and have been retired for at least five. Lancashire's trio of rugby league greats, with their places of birth and clubs, are:

Alex Murphy
(born in St Helens; played for St Helens, Leigh and Warrington)
Vince Karalius
(born in Widnes; played for St Helens and Widnes)
Eric Ashton
(born in St Helens; played for Wigan)

꒤꒤꒤꒤꒤꒤꒤꒤꒤꒤꒤꒤꒤꒤꒤꒤꒤꒤꒤꒤꒤꒤

DANIEL DEFOE ON LANCASHIRE

Daniel Defoe is best known for his novels including *Robinson Crusoe*, but between 1724 and 1727 he undertook perhaps his most significant wo rk of non-fiction: *A Tour Through the Whole Island of Great Britain*. His survey of the country included a long visit to Lancashire and these observations on its places.

On Liverpool

Liverpool is one of the wonders of Britain... the town was, at my first visiting it, a large, handsome, well built and increasing or thriving town... and I am told that it still visibly increases both in wealth, people, business and buildings. What it may grow to in time, I know not... In a word, there is no town in England, London excepted, that can equal Liverpool for the fineness of the streets, and beauty of the buildings.

On Manchester

Manchester is one of the greatest, if not really the greatest mere village in England. It is neither a walled town, city or corporation; they send no members to Parliament; and the highest magistrate they have is a constable. And yet it has a collegiate church, several parishes, takes up a large space of ground, and, including the suburb, it is said to contain above fifty thousand people.

On Bolton

About eight miles from Manchester, northwest, lies Bolton... We saw nothing remarkable in this town, but that the cotton manufacture reached hither; but the place did not, like Manchester, seem so flourishing and increasing.

On Preston

Preston is a fine town, and tolerably full of people, but not like Liverpool or Manchester; besides, we come now beyond the trading part of the county. Here is no manufacture; the town is full of attorneys, proctors and notaries, the process of law here being of a different nature than they are in other places, it being a duchy and county palatine, and having particular privileges of its own. The people are gay here, though not perhaps the richer for that; but it has by that obtained the name of Proud Preston.

On Lancaster

Lancaster is the county town, and situated near the mouth of the River Lune. The town is ancient; it lies, as it were, in its own ruins, and has little to recommend it but a decayed castle and a more decayed port... the bridge is handsome and strong, but, as before, here is little or no trade, and few people... This part of the country seemed very strange to us... for here we were, as it were, locked in between the hills on one side high as the clouds, and prodigiously higher, and the sea on the other, and the sea itself seemed desolate and wild, for it was a sea without ships, here being no sea port or place of trade.

On the hills of the Furness region

They were, in my thoughts, monstrous high; but in a country all mountainous and full of innumerable high hills, it was not easy for a traveller to judge which was highest. Nor were these hills high and formidable only, but they had a kind of an unhospitable terror in them. Here were no rich pleasant valleys between them, as among the Alps; no lead mines and veins of rich oar, as in the Peak; no coal pits, as in the hills about Halifax, much less gold, as in the Andes, but all barren and wild, of no use or advantage either to man or beast.

LAND USE IN LANCASHIRE

Perhaps surprisingly for what is, in many parts, a densely populated county, more than four fifths of Lancashire is green. Of the 800,327 acres (323,881 ha) within the current administrative boundaries of the county, 659,440 (266,866 ha) of them – or 82.4 per cent – are covered by green space. That compares to 88 per cent for England as a whole. The proportion of green space varies enormously across the county – from 29 per cent in Blackpool to 95 per cent in the Ribble Valley.

In addition, 53,585 acres (21,685 ha) of Lancashire (or 6.7 per cent of its total) are covered by water – though much of this is encroaching coastal water rather than lakes or ponds. That leaves less than one acre in ten across the county covered by man-made developments like buildings, paths and roads.

800,327 . . . . total acres (323,881 ha) in Lancashire

659,440 . . . . acres (266,866 ha) covered by green space
(82.4 per cent of total)

53,585 . . . . acres (21,685 ha) covered by water (6.7 per cent)

32,716 . . . . acres (13,240 ha) covered by paths (4.1 per cent)

21,829 . . . . acres (8,834 ha) covered by non-domestic buildings
(2.7 per cent)

11,302 . . . . acres (4,574 ha) covered by domestic buildings
(1.4 per cent)

6,640 . . . . acres (2,687 ha) covered by domestic gardens
(0.8 per cent)

1,146 . . . . acres (464 ha) covered by roads (0.1 per cent)

1,053 . . . . acres (426 ha) covered by railways (0.1 per cent)

12,620 . . . . acres (5,107 ha) covered by other surfaces
(1.6 per cent)

THE LANCASHIRE PALS

Of the many poignant stories of Lancashire's role in the First World War, some of the most affecting relate to the county's 'Pals Battalions' – groups of men from local towns and cities who signed up and fought in the war together.

The regiments were the idea of Lord Kitchener, Secretary of State for War, who realised that inviting friends or workmates to join the forces alongside one another would be a more socially and politically expedient recruitment tactic than immediate conscription. It worked, and towns across the country were soon competing to outdo each other in recruits and prove themselves the country's most patriotic places. The first place in the country to sign up enough men for a Pals Battalion – typically around a thousand – was Liverpool, following an appeal by the Earl of Derby within days of Kitchener issuing his plea. The city went on to contribute three more Battalions, a total matched by Salford and exceeded by Manchester, which raised eight. Perhaps because civic pride was high here – or perhaps because army life seemed to offer an appealing escape from the widespread poverty and misery of life in its industrial towns – Lancashire was particularly fertile ground for the army, and had returned dozens of Pals Battalions by the end of 1914.

Most spent more than a year training for service before being dispatched to the front, where the realities of the war became terrifyingly apparent. Many of the battalions were thrown into the Battle of the Somme and immediately suffered terrible casualties, with some all but wiped out overnight. Because the men of the battalions had, by their nature, all hailed from the same localities, the effect of the losses on their home towns was enormous. Accrington, for instance – the smallest town in the whole country to form a Pals Battalion – had 720 men fighting on the first day of the Somme, and suffered 584 killed or wounded. Of those who survived the battle and others afterwards, many were absorbed into the regular army for the rest of the war. The catastrophic impact on individual communities meant that the Pals Battalions were not repeated during the Second World War.

Memorials to Lancashire's Pals Battalions can be found in all of the towns and cities that sent them, as well as at many war graves and battle sites in France. Some towns, including Accrington, continue to hold memorial services for their men every year.

LANCASHIRE POEMS –
'THE WAYVER OF WELLBROOK'

Like many of the best Lancashire dialect poets of the 19th century, Ben Brierley was almost entirely self-taught. Born in Failsworth, between Manchester and Oldham, he started working as a bobbin winder for his father while still a young boy, picking up education wherever he could and before long writing sketches and poems in both standard English and dialect for local publications. He later launched his own journal and gave public readings of his work, his fame having spread as far as the US, which he toured twice to the delight of nostalgic Lancashire ex-pats there. Failsworth today has a statue commemorating him.

One of Brierley's best known poems is 'The Wayver of Wellbrook' (a fictional place), which sets up a contrast between Lancashire's humble handloom weavers and the landed gentry. Its celebration of simple values, self-sufficiency and a contented life would have struck a chord with Lancashire's working classes, and with a bouncy chorus and simple rhythms it was clearly written to be sung rather than read – perhaps while the singer worked away on his or her loom.

Yo' gentlemen o with yo'r heaunds an' yo'r parks –
Yo' may gamble an' sport till yo' dee;
Bo a quiet heause nook, a good wife, an' a book,
Is mooar to the likins o' me.

Chorus: Wi' mi pickers an' pins,
An' my wellers to th' shins;
Mi linderins, shuttle and yealdhook;
Mi treddles an' sticks;
Mi weight-ropes an' bricks;
What a life! said the wayver o' Wellbrook.

Aw care no' for titles, nor heauses, nor lond;
Owd Jone's a name fittin' for me;
An' gi' me a thatch wi' a wooden dur-latch,
An' six feet o' greaund when aw dee.
Wi' mi pickers etc.

Some folk like t'stuff their owd wallets wi' mayte,
Till they're as round an' as brawsen as frogs;
But for me, aw'm content, when aw've paid deawn mi rent,
Wi' enoof t'keep me up i' mi clogs.
Wi' mi pickers etc.

An' ther some are too idle to use their own feet,
An' mun keawer an' stroddle i' th'lone;
But when awm wheel't or carried it'll be to get burried,
An' then Dicky-up wi' owd Jone.
Wi' mi pickers etc.

Yo' may turn up yo'r noses at me an' th'owd dame,
An' thrutch us like dogs agen th' wo;
Bo as long as aw can naygur, aw'll ne'er be a beggar,
So aw care no' a cuss for yo.
Wi' mi pickers etc.

Then Margit, turn reaund that owd hum-a-drum wheel,
An' mi shuttle shall fly like a brid;
An' when aw no longer con use hont or finger,
They'n say while aw could do aw did.
Wi' mi pickers etc.

Glossary: *o* (line 1) means all; *heaunds* (1) means hounds; *heause* (3) means house; *pickers, pins* (5), *wellers* (6), *linderins, shuttle, yealdhook* (7), *treddles* (8) and *weight-ropes* (9) are all parts or instruments on a loom; *wayver* (10) means weaver; *wallets* (15) means stomachs; *mayte* (15) means meat; *brawsen* (16) means full; *keaver* (20) means cower (as in sit in a carriage); *stroddle* (20) means straddle (a horse); *Dicky-up* (22) means dead; *thrutch* (24) means push; *wo* (24) means wall; *naygur* (25) means work; *hum-a-drum wheel* (27) means spinning wheel; *brid* (28) means bird; *hont* (29) means hand.

ROADS IN LANCASHIRE

There are some 5,030 miles (8,050 km) of roads in the modern administrative county of Lancashire, excluding chunks of it now dassified elsewhere like Manchester and Liverpool. That number is made up of 107 miles (172 km) of motorway; 309 and 189 miles (497 and 304 km) of rural and urban A roads; 2,043 and 2,308 miles (3,288 and 3,714 km) of rural and urban minor roads; and a few more miles of unclassified stretches.

Put end to end, Lancashire's roads would stretch around the entire coastline of Great Britain. To fill them all, in 2008 there were some 655,000 vehicles registered in Lancashire – made up of 544,000 cars, 25,000 motorcycles, 57,000 light goods vehicles, 13,000 heavy goods vehicles, 3,000 buses and coaches and 13,000 other vehicles. These vehicles traveled an estimated 7,135 million miles (11,483 million km) in 2008. Road casualty figures in Lancashire are slightly higher than the national average at around five people injured in some way per 1,000 population. A total of 929 people were killed or seriously injured on Lancashire's roads in 2008, and 7,199 people suffered injuries of all severities, including minor ones.

Lancashire boasts a number of firsts and records in road history. It is home to the UK's first ever motorway – the 8-mile (13 km) Preston bypass that was opened in 1958 and that grew into the M6, now the country's longest motorway. It has the UK's highest stretch of motorway – a piece of the M62 near the Lancashire-Yorkshire border that reaches more than 1,200 feet (366 m) above sea level. And it was the first part of the country – and probably the world – to introduce white lines in the middle of roads.

UNUSUAL MOUNTAIN RESCUES

Lancashire's various mountain rescue teams all keep logs, meticulously recording the details of every call-out they attend. The roll-calls of stranded walkers, all-night searches, broken bones and occasional fatalities make for alarming reading, reminding of the perils of Lancashire's wild country. But while each call-out involves the mobilisation of entirely voluntary rescuers, often in the middle of the night and the depths of winter, not all of the incidents turn out to be so serious. Here are ten of the more intriguing entries from the Lancashire log books of the Bowland Pennine, Rossendale and Pendle, Coniston and Kendal mountain rescue teams in the last few years.

7 July 2009. Two young lads reported hearing distress whistles. Turned out to be a peregrine falcon. *Coniston Mountain Rescue Team*

19 June 2009. The team were asked to assist the Fire Service who had been called to rescue a cow from a stream at Cartmel who had been there all night, unable to move. A local farmer with a tractor with a rear board reversed up the stream and the cow was rolled on to the board and strapped down. The cow was taken to a nearby farm to enable a vet to examine her. *Kendal Mountain Search and Rescue Team*

6 April 2009. Request to search for a patient missing from a local hospital. Team Incident Controller immediately dispatched to hospital to liaise with Police Search Manager and confirm that a thorough search of the hospital had been undertaken. It was decided to dispatch the team's trailing dog unit to determine if the person had left the building and ascertain a direction of travel. Team soon stood down when person found locked in a cupboard within the building! *Bowland Pennine Mountain Rescue Team*

1 April 2009. We were called to help a paraglider reportedly crashed on Pendle Big End. The pilot had gone onto the hillside and spread his canopy, and was awaiting sufficient breeze for take-off. The canopy was seen by a group of walkers who assumed it was a crash and alerted the ambulance. A team member, who was running in the area, introduced himself to the ambulance crew who where gazing toward the summit. He took one of their phones and ran up to the 'casualty' site to find the pilot fit and well and enjoying the spectacle below. *Rossendale and Pendle Mountain Rescue Team*

30 December 2008. Public reported possible orange bivvy bag up a ghyll. Found to be a discarded lilo. *Coniston Mountain Rescue Team*

16 May 2008. Team leader received request from a Lancashire Police Search Advisor as to the availability of our trailing dog unit. A three-year-old boy had been missing for some hours in Blackburn town centre. Trailing dog unit stood down when the good news came that the lad had been found, safe, having apparently got on a bus and taken a trip to Bolton and back. *Bowland Pennine Mountain Rescue Team*

23 February 2008. Man walking on Coniston Old Man / Swirl How Man reported missing by friends. Search commenced from Levers Water when notification was received that he had been located enjoying a pint in a pub in Broughton. *Coniston Mountain Rescue Team*

7 June 2007. Request by Lancashire Fire and Rescue Service to assist with an animal rescue - a sheep on a mill roof! The animal was 'encouraged' to move to safety by firefighters and team members. *Rossendale and Pendle Mountain Rescue Team*

5 May 2007. Team paged by Lancashire Police to urgently attend Brindle Quarry where a 14-year-old girl, somewhat worse for drink, was reported as 'stuck'. However, the team was immediately stood down as the first police officer on scene had been able to recover the young lady. *Bowland Pennine Mountain Rescue Team*

21 January 2007. Team received a request from Lancashire Ambulance Service for assistance in moving an overweight person from a house in Skelmersdale for transfer to hospital. As this is not the type of work we normally undertake it was suggested that they contact the Fire and Rescue Service. *Bowland Pennine Mountain Rescue Team*

PRISONER OF WAR CAMPS

There were prisoner of war camps in 11 locations across Lancashire during the Second World War. Most were hurriedly adapted from existing buildings into emergency camps as the Allied forces increased their number of enemy prisoners. They included a couple, in Oldham and Bury, that were modified from cotton mills and weaving sheds, as well as old stately homes, parks, farms and youth hostels. The 11 sites were:

Glen Mill, Oldham

Warth Mills, Bury

Ormskirk

Garswood Park, Ashton-in-Makerfield

Bank Hall, Bretherton, Preston

Melland Camp, Gorton, Manchester

Newton Camp, Newton-with-Scales, Kirkham

Brookmill Camp, Woodlands, Kirkham

Knowsley Park, Prescot

Penketh Hostel, Barrow's Green, Widnes

Fort Crosby, Hightown

As is the case across the country, few remains of the camps now exist, since most either reverted to their former use or were knocked down after the end of the war. Some decaying buildings and fences can still be seen, notably at Fort Crosby in the village of Hightown on the coast north of Liverpool.

LANCASHIRE INDUSTRY – PORTS, SHIPS AND FISHING

For several centuries, the history of parts of Lancashire like Liverpool was inextricably tied to the fortunes of its ports and the trading opportunities that they opened up.

Although fishing and very small-scale trade was probably conducted from Liverpool right from its foundation, it was the second half of the

17th century that brought it to the fore. The first trans-Atlantic cargo arrived there in 1648, and Liverpool was soon sending goods like textiles back from the county in exchange for imports like sugar. With the arrival of the horrific slave trade, growth was soon exponential, and by 1715 Liverpool had become the world's first commercial wet dock, at which ships could unload straight to the quay rather than via secondary boats.

The fortunes earned from slavery and trading transformed Liverpool, the population rising from a few thousand at the start of the 18th century to around 80,000 at the end of it. Inspired by its success, other Lancashire towns tried to develop ports and trades of their own, and Lancaster used the slave trade to establish itself as a particularly important centre via satellite ports at places like Glasson, Heysham and Sunderland Point. Associated industries like shipbuilding and repairing flourished too, with Merseyside boasting thriving shipyards.

Liverpool was set back for a while by restrictions on trade caused by the American War of Independence and the abolition of slavery, but the Industrial Revolution saw the city boom again. It was a hub for Lancashire's cotton industry, and was bolstered still further by the opening of canal and railway links to the rest of the county and beyond. Steamships started up regular liner services across the Atlantic from the 1840s, and attracted by the opportunities for work, immigrants flooded in, notably from Ireland. By the 1890s, Liverpool was Britain's second biggest port after London, and docks stretched for more than 10 miles (16 km) along the Mersey.

The port inevitably declined through the 20th century, hit by a combination of a global decline in trade, two world wars and competition from rail, road and air transport. But while traffic and job numbers have fallen dramatically from its golden age, the volume of cargo it handles has remained more steady at around 32 million tons a year – about 6 per cent of the UK's total. Other Lancashire ports like Fleetwood and Heysham have suffered steeper declines, though both still join Liverpool in providing passenger ferry services across to Ireland and the Isle of Man. Shipbuilding has fallen in the face of foreign competition too, though Barrow-in-Furness remains an important centre for the manufacture of military craft.

Lancashire ports including Fleetwood have also been closely associated with fishing over the centuries, and this at one time was the most important long-distance fishing port on the whole of England's west coast, responsible for between two and three thousand jobs. Nowadays the total numbers of both workers and registered fishing vessels are down to two figures, though Fleetwood remains an important centre for the processing and auctioning of fish caught from other ports. But like many coastal, riverside and canalside towns in

Lancashire, any boats found here nowadays are likely to be owned for pleasure trips than for business. Rejuvenation of the county's ports focuses on marina developments and housing, office, retail and leisure markets rather than fishing or freight transport – a situation that as little as a century ago would have been inconceivable.

Good places to learn more about Lancashire's seafaring history include the Merseyside Maritime Museum on Albert Dock (tel 0151 478 4499 or visit www.liverpoolmuseums.org.uk) and the Lancaster Maritime Museum on St George's Quay (tel 01524 382264 or visit www.lancashire.gov.uk), as well as the Fleetwood Museum (tel 01253 876621 or visit www.lancashire.gov.uk) and the Fleetwood Online Archive of Trawlers (neatly abbreviated to FLOAT), a nostalgia-filled library of trawlers that have operated from this and other ports (visit http://float-trawlers.lancashire.gov.uk).

LANCASHIRE FOOD – BLACKPOOL ROCK

If it doesn't break them first, seaside rock in Blackpool and other resorts is likely to rot your teeth. But it is also an essential ingredient of the Lancashire seaside holiday – as integral a part of summer on the beach as donkey rides, ice cream and rain.

With sugar cane imported across the Atlantic into ports on the northwest coast like Liverpool, Lancashire was a natural home for boiled sweets like rock. (It has also created other sugary treats like jelly babies, made for the first time in Nelson, and Fisherman's Friend tablets, invented and still made in Fleetwood.) Seaside resorts adopted sweets like rock as they grew in popularity, and it was certainly here, towards the end of the 19th century, that the novelty of lettering in rock was embraced by retailers and holidaymakers. Its pioneers include Ben Bullock, a Lancashire-born sweet-maker who is thought to have been the first to incorporate the words 'Blackpool Rock', and Dick Taylor, a Blackpool shop owner who was among the early retailers of the new confection.

While its basic recipe may be simple, the job of running lettering through to create the classic seaside rock is much more fiddly. Rock makers first boil up sugar, glucose syrup and water in large copper pans, and mix in a few flavourings like mint as it cools in slabs to a dough-like consistency. Pulling machines then churn and aerate the mixture, which is divided into batches that will form the inner, outer and lettering components of the rock. Each is usually coloured differently, often in a variety of lurid pinks.

Each letter is hand-formed individually from the coloured mixture in blocks several feet long. They are then arranged together to spell out whatever word is required, each letter carefully separated by spacers of white rock. An outer layer of rock is then wrapped around this core, and water wiped on to bind everything together. The large cylinder of sugar 'dough', by now weighing up to 50 kg, is pulled slowly through rollers, gradually reducing its circumference to between half an inch and an inch, and producing a long string of still warm rock. Cut to size – usually around 12 inches or a foot – it is finally left to cool and harden before being wrapped in cellophane. Because of this last rolling and stretching process, makers' lettering is formed much larger than it appears on the finished rock, but it is nevertheless a skilled job that takes years to master.

Rock's heyday was probably in the 1950s and 1960s, when the great British seaside resorts like Blackpool boomed and it offered a cheap and easy gift for holidaymakers returning home. Foreign holidays and dental health warnings might have reduced its popularity since, but it can still be found in every other shopfront along the coast at Blackpool and elsewhere, and it is increasingly popular as a corporate promotional gift and wedding favour. Throughout its history, it has remained a curiously British phenomenon, eaten virtually nowhere else in the world.

THE LOST LAKE

These days the largest lake in Lancashire is Windermere, which forms the border with Westmorland in the far north of the historic county. Measuring around 10 miles (16 km) from top to bottom and with a surface area of nearly 6 square miles (16 sq km), it is also the largest natural lake in England.

Further south in the county, however, lies the site of a lake that was almost certainly much bigger than Windermere. Martin Mere, on the edge of Burscough near Ormskirk, was formed at the end of the last Ice Age when retreating glaciers left a water-filled depression. Its levels rose and fell over the centuries and records of its surface area vary enormously as a result, but several sources put its size at 8 to 10 square miles (20 to 26 sq km) at various times. Efforts to drain the mere and reclaim its rich peat pastures were made over the 18th and 19th centuries, and while they were ultimately successful heavy rainfall reclaimed the lake for short periods right up to the 1950s.

Martin Mere is now looked after by the Wildfowl and Wetlands Trust, which ironically now sometimes floods rather than drains the site to maintain its habitats. As in the past, it is home to hundreds of species of plants, mammals and birds, including rare ducks, geese, swans and flamingos. It is open to the public 364 days a year (tel 01704 895181 or visit www.wwt.org.uk/martinmere).

One of the lake's other claims to fame is that it was the enchanted lake into which King Arthur's legendary sword Excalibur was thrown. As with most stories associated with Arthur, however, the legend of its location is somewhat vague, and numerous other lakes have been claimed as its home, especially in Wales and southwest England.

LANCASHIRE'S MANUFACTURING IN NUMBERS

Ever since the Industrial Revolution, Lancashire has been one of the leading manufacturing counties of the UK. These figures show the value of manufacturing to the local workforce and economy.

320,000 . . . estimated number of people employed in manufacturing in Lancashire at its peak in the early 1910s

280,000 . . . estimated number of people employed in manufacturing in the 1950s

102,500 . . . estimated number of people employed in manufacturing in 2007

79,800 . . . . number of these people who are male

16.5 . . . . percentage of Lancashire's total workforce employed in manufacturing

11 . . . . percentage of England's total workforce employed in manufacturing

4,293 . . . . businesses involved in manufacturing in Lancashire

88 . . . . number of these businesses with more than 200 staff

3,168 . . . . number of these businesses with ten or fewer staff

13.7 . . . . total annual turnover in billions of pounds of manufacturing firms

5.1 . . . . Gross Value Added total in billions of pounds of the manufacturing industry in Lancashire (value of goods produced minus materials' cost)

26,900 . . . . Average annual salary in pounds in manufacturing in Lancashire

In 2007, Lancashire's top ten manufacturing sectors by employee numbers were:

1 Non-motor transport equipment
   (mostly aerospace; 19,900 staff)
2 Food and drink (13,000)
3 Non-machinery metal products (9,220)
4 Machinery and equipment (8,300)
5= Furniture (7,100)
5= Rubber and plastic (7,100)
7 Chemicals and chemical products (6,200)
8 Publishing and printing (5,600)
9= Textiles (4,600)
9= Motor vehicles (4,600)

HORSE RACING AND THE GRAND NATIONAL

Perhaps surprisingly for such a large county, Lancashire has only three racecourses: Aintree in Liverpool, Cartmel in the southern Lake District and Haydock Park near Newton-le-Willows. But while its facilities suffer by comparison with other counties - Yorkshire, for instance, has nine courses - Lancashire can claim to be home to the greatest single race in the sport: the Grand National.

Nowadays the Aintree course draws around 70,000 spectators for Grand National Day, with hundreds of millions more watching on TV and some £80 million staked on the outcome, but the race's origins are much more humble. It grew out of a popular hare race organised by a Liverpool innkeeper, William Lynn, who moved into horseracing by leasing ground at Aintree from the Earl of Sefton, known locally as Lord Dashalong because of his fondness for the sport. A local event at first, it built a following further afield, aided by the arrival in the town of the railway and the addition to the course of hurdles. The first Aintree Grand National proper - though known then as the Grand Liverpool Steeplechase - was held in 1839 and won - appropriately enough given the amount of luck required by jockeys to complete the course, let alone win it - by a horse called Lottery.

A succession of dramatic races soon established the race as one of the leading jump events in the country, and except during the two world wars, it has been staged at Aintree every year since. That first race featured large stretches of ploughed land and brooks, ditches and a stone wall as jumps, and although things have since been made a little safer it remains a hugely challenging course, run over two laps of a gruelling 16-fence circuit totalling some 4.5 miles (7 km). More than 50 horses have died in Grand Nationals since 1990, and the race is often targeted by animal rights protestors as a result. Other recent controversies have included the 1993 race, declared void after a false start; and a two-day delay to the 1997 edition following a bomb scare at the course.

Some Grand National records

66 . . . . the most horses starting a race, in 1929

23 . . . . the most horses finishing a race, in 1984

2 . . . . the fewest horses finishing a race, in 1928

8 . . . . the most starts by a horse – Manifesto

3 . . . . the most wins by a horse – Red Rum

5 . . . . the most wins by a jockey – George Stevens

4 . . . . . the most wins by a trainer – Fred Rimmell and Ginger McCain

17 . . . . the age of the youngest winning jockey – Bruce Hobbs

48 . . . . the age of the oldest winning jockey – Dick Saunders

528 . . . . the fastest winning time in seconds, by Mr Frisk in 1990

100–1 . . . . the longest odds by a winner – achieved five times,
most recently by Mon Mome in 2009

A LANCASHIRE DICTIONARY PART THREE: P TO Z

A final guide to words from the Lancashire vocabulary and their meanings, to help make you fluent in the local lingo.

pad path
perish to freeze
pobs or **pobbies** bread and milk
popped his or **her clogs** died
pother smoke
pouce a naughty child
powfagged very tired
powse rubbish, useless material

prato potato
puddle to confuse
punce to kick
purrit put it
puttybrains simpleton

rake to scratch
rant a wild time, often involving drink

reet right
right misery a very miserable person
rip rap firework; also an excitable child
ripstitch exuberant, reckless person
rive to tear
roach coal pit
ruckle to disturb

sad heavy, solid; as in sad cake
sauce impudence
scrannel of poor quality
scutch to beat
sen self
sennit a week; literally seven nights
shape to do something properly
shift to move
shive slice, usually of bread
shop place; as in 'all over the shop'
shut to get rid of
sich such
side to clear up, tidy
sithee look you; or a 'see you' farewell
sken squint
skrike to cry out
slammock to walk awkwardly
slance to steal
slatt'at drunk
slatterins left-overs
slutch mud
snod smooth
snortch to sneeze
sny crowded
sope a drop
soss to throw down
sossingers sausages

speyk speak
stond stand
strap credit
summat something

t' the
talkin' bang speaking standard English
talkin' broad speaking Lancashire dialect
tally to live in sin
tarra goodbye
tek take
that so; as in 'it were that cheap'
thee you
threap to fight or argue
thrutch to move restlessly
tiff or **tift** quarrel
tollering showing off

up t'stick pregnant
us our

vast very

wamble to shake violently
wark pain
watter water
we's our
welly well-nigh, nearly
wheer where
whisk tail a woman of ill repute
whoam home
whorr what
wi' with
wick quick, lively

yammer to long for
yer hear, listen
yersel yourself
yon yonder

TEN CHURCHES

Lancashire has a rich stock of parish churches. Here are ten of the most interesting.

All Hallow's Church, Great Mitton

One of the best preserved and interesting medieval churches in England, let alone Lancashire. Dramatically located close to where the Rivers Ribble and Hodder meet, its features include a sloping nave and a chapel built for the Sherburne family.

St Ann's Church, Manchester

Manchester was a small rural town when this church was consecrated in 1712, and it has watched the city's incredible growth all around it ever since. Built in the neo-classical style from local sandstone, its interior was added to throughout the 19th century.

Cartmel Priory

The 12th-century priory that was built here by Augustinian canons dominates the Lake District – but also Lancashire – village of Cartmel. The nearby gatehouse to the priory is looked after by the National Trust.

St Helen's Church, Overton

South of Morecambe near the Lune Estuary, St Helen's is usually credited as the oldest church building in Lancashire. It was founded around 1050, and while it has been added to over the centuries, original elements like the door and walls survive.

St Helen's Church, Sefton

The only Grade I listed building in Sefton and one of the oldest buildings anywhere in Merseyside, this church can trace its history back to 1170 when it was consecrated as a family chapel, though most of what is there now dates to the 16th century. It is particularly renowned for its Tudor woodwork.

St Leonard's Church, Middleton

There was a wooden Saxon and then a Norman church on this site before St Leonard's was restored by Sir Richard Assheton after the 1513 Battle of Flodden Field, by way of thanks to Middleton archers who had saved his life. It has a stained glass window commemorating the 17 men.

St Mary's Church, Whalley

Situated next to the spectacular ruins of Whalley Abbey, this church is
mentioned in the Domesday Book and has three Anglo-Saxon crosses
in the graveyard. Features include carved bosses in the oak roof,
a 13th-century Priest's Door and well preserved misericords.

St Michael and All Angels Church, Hawkshead

Lancashire's northernmost church, this has a picturesque setting
above the village with the Lakeland fells all around. It was built
around 1500, and the bell tower is the oldest surviving element.

St Walburge's Church, Preston

Gothic-inspired Roman Catholic church near the River Ribble in
Preston, built in the mid-19th century. It is notable for its 300-feet
(91 m) spire, the highest of any parish church in England and the
third highest of all after Salisbury and Norwich cathedrals.

St Wilfrid's Church, Standish

Rated by the famous architectural scholar Nikolaus Pevsner as one of
Lancashire's most interesting churches, St Wilfrid's as it stands was
built in the Gothic and Renaissance styles in the late 16th century,
though churches have existed on this spot since the 12th.

BRITAIN'S MOST DANGEROUS STREET

From the night Lancashire's favourite TV soap opera first screened in
December 1960, *Coronation Street* has rarely been short of dramatic
storylines. There have been some 40 births, 70 weddings and 35 divorces
over the show's five decades, but most memorable to many viewers
have been the startlingly frequent deaths on the Street – a total of more
than 110 at an average of more than two a year.

The first character to go was May Hardman, who died of a brain
tumour just three weeks after that first episode. Since then around
30 people have died of perhaps the most dramatic on-screen death, a
heart attack or failure, and around a dozen from old age or natural
causes. But one of the biggest killers on the soap has been traffic – the
cause of nearly 30 deaths since Ida Barlow was hit by a bus in 1961.
Accidents involving cars, lorries, trucks, vans and trams have all made
Wetherfield Lancashire's most dangerous town for drivers and
pedestrians alike. There have also been more than a dozen murders, five
suicides and an array of unfortunate accidents.

Around half of *Coronation Street*'s deaths have occurred since 1995, since when scriptwriters have developed increasingly imaginative final storylines for major and minor characters. Here are ten of the most unusual and dramatic deaths in *Coronation Street's* history.

1971 Valerie Barlow. Electrocuted by her hairdryer after trying to fix some dodgy wiring.

1976 Ernest Bishop. Accidentally shot dead in a bungled raid on Mike Baldwin's clothing factory.

1984 Stan Ogden. Probably the only character in TV soap history to die of gangrene.

1989 Alan Bradley. Knocked down by a tram on Blackpool promenade.

1991 Amy Burton. Suffered a heart attack while playing bingo.

1992 Ted Sullivan. Another heart attack victim, this time suffered while watching Percy Sugden play bowls.

1998 Annie Malone. The assistant manager at Firman's Freezers froze to death after being accidentally locked in a freezer.

1999 Judy Mallett. Suffered a pulmonary embolism while pegging out the washing.

2000 Dean Sykes. Shot by a police marksman following a siege that began when he tried to hold up a supermarket till.

2005 Katy Harris. A diabetic who committed suicide by the ingenious method of eating spoonfuls of sugar.

ROOM OCCUPANCY RATES

When is the best time to visit Lancashire? Based on room occupancy rates across the modern administrative county, the quietest months are the first of the year, when fewer than half all beds are filled; and the busiest are August and October, when two in three are taken. The figures below are from tourist boards' surveys of room occupancy in serviced accommodation – hotels, B&Bs and guesthouses – and indicate how difficult it is likely to be to find a room for the night at any given time. Occupancy rates in both Liverpool and Manchester are much higher all year round, reflecting the volume of business visits to the cities.

Room occupancy in percentage in 2008

Month	Lancashire	Liverpool	Manchester
January	45	59	68
February	45	67	76
March	46	71	79
April	46	72	73
May	55	72	78
June	48	73	79
July	58	74	77
August	64	73	67
September	57	79	79
October	64	77	80
November	47	75	83
December	46	64	74

GREAT LANCASTRIANS – GRACIE FIELDS

From a fish and chip shop in Rochdale to national superstardom and a damehood, no Lancastrian has followed the rags to riches path quite so spectacularly as Gracie Fields.

She was born Grace Stansfield, in a terraced house above her grandmother's shop in 1898. Encouraged by a theatrical family, she was appearing on stage by the age of seven, and touring the music halls of Lancashire and beyond by her teens – though like many in Rochdale she also worked for a while in one of the countless local cotton mills. Her early work under her adopted and intentionally more glamorous name included revue shows with her first husband and manager, a comedian called Archie Pitt, and it was when one of these transferred to London's West End in the early 1920s that her career really took off. Her popularity owed much to her image as a forthright, effervescent Lancastrian, and she played up to this with a variety act that mixed easy-going songs, monologues and jokes. She was adored by the working classes, who recognised her as one of their own and true to her roots.

Playing at sold-out halls around the country brought Fields to the attention of those in the emerging talking pictures or 'talkies' industry, and she transferred successfully to film. For much of the 1930s she was Britain's leading box office star, appearing in more than a dozen films in the UK and US before withdrawing after being diagnosed with cervical cancer in 1939.

Although she recovered – and claimed to have received more than quarter of a million messages of goodwill from the British public as she did so – Fields' popularity then started to decline. By now living on Capri and married to an Italian-born film director, she left the UK after her husband's country entered the Second World War, and although she supported the war effort from their new homes in the US and Canada, frequently entertained Allied troops and often returned home to England, she was criticised by some for deserting her country.

Fields continued her musical and stage careers after the war, though she substantially reduced her workload and did not return to films. And while her appearances in England became fewer, she remained hugely popular in Lancashire, the county she did so much to personify. She is particularly well remembered in Rochdale, of which she was awarded the freedom in 1938, and returned there a year before she died in the late 1970s to open its Gracie Fields Theatre.

A DIARY OF FARMERS' MARKETS

The rising interest in locally produced food has been a rare bit of good news for farmers in Lancashire, and the trend has led to a huge increase in the number of farmers' markets across the county. Providing more profit for farmers than selling through the big supermarkets, these local markets also present an opportunity for food producers and shoppers to meet one another face to face – and they are great places to pick up some of the local food of which Lancashire is rightly proud. Here is a selection of 35 of the biggest and best farmers' markets in Lancashire, typically open from nine or ten in the morning until the early afternoon.

Ashton-under-Lyne – last Sunday of the month at the Market Hall
Bentham – first Saturday of the month at the Town Hall
Bolton – fourth Sunday of the month on Victoria Square
Burscough – second Sunday of the month at the Older People's Club
Carnforth – fourth Wednesday of the month at the Station
Chorley – third Thursday of every other month on Market Street

Clitheroe – first and third Tuesday of the month on Moor Lane
Colne – third Saturday of the month on Market Street
Fleetwood – third Friday of the month at the Market
Garstang – first Tuesday of the month on the High Street
Great Eccleston – third Wednesday of the month on The Square
Grimsargh – third Saturday of the month at the Village Hall
Heysham – second Friday of the month at St James' Church
Hoghton – third Sunday of the month at Hoghton Tower
Lancaster – second Saturday of the month on Market Square
Leyburn – fourth Saturday of the month on Market Place
Liverpool – second Saturday of the month at Woolton Village; third
   Sunday of the month on Hope Street; fourth Saturday of the month
   on Lark Lane
Manchester – second and fourth Friday and Saturday of the month
   at Piccadilly Gardens
Mawdesley – first Saturday of the month at Cedar Farm
Oldham – second Sunday of the month at Saddleworth Museum
Penwortham – first Saturday of the month in St Mary's Church Hall
Poulton-le-Fylde – fourth Saturday of the month on Vicarage Road
Preston – second Saturday of the month at Preston Markets
Ramsbottom – second Saturday of the month on Market Place
Rochdale – first Sunday of the month on Market Place
Rossendale – first Sunday of the month at Helmshore Mills
   Textile Museum
Samlesbury – last Sunday of the month at Samlesbury Hall
Scarisbrick – second Tuesday of the month at the Village Hall
Southport – last Thursday of the month on King Street
Standish – last Saturday of the month at the Community Centre
St Annes – first Thursday of the month on The Square
Thornton – second Saturday of the month at Marsh Mill
Ulverston – third Saturday of the month at the Market Hall
Whalley – last Sunday of the month at The Swan Inn
Wigan – first Tuesday of the month at the Outdoor Market

HOW TO BUILD A CAIRN

Anyone who has walked any distance on the Lancashire fells will have
encountered cairns – piles of stones marking the summits or placed
as guides along the paths for people walking up or down. When the
mist descends and visibility shortens, they can be important markers to
anyone struggling to find their way.

Many walkers follow the tradition of adding stones to cairns as they pass them, and some large piles have accumulated on popular routes, especially in the southern Lake District. Most of these are fairly ragged affairs, but occasionally much neater assemblies can be found, purpose-built by dry stone wallers and demonstrating the distinctive art of cairn sculpture. Builders start, as they do when planning a wall, by picking the right position – a firm, fairly flat base – and gathering a large quantity of stones of similar size and shape. The cairn begins with a circular base, the outer ring of which requires the largest stones, with the widest ends of them to the outside. The middle of the base – the 'heart' of the cairn – is filled with smaller stones, packed tightly. Now the cairn is built upwards like a cone, stones added neatly and slowly to fit in with the rest and build up its strength. Each layer is kept as flat and tight as possible, with smaller stones used as the cairn rises. The top stone is the neatest and shiniest of them all.

LANCASHIRE'S LEAST AND MOST AFFORDABLE TOWNS

Ormskirk and Carnforth are the least affordable towns in which to live in Lancashire, and Nelson and Bootle the most affordable. These top tens are based on the house prices of postal towns according to the Halifax House Price Index, which monitors the average selling prices of properties across the country, and their relative affordability for key workers like teachers and nurses. So while average house prices in Ormskirk are more than seven times the average salary of a key worker, for instance, in Nelson the multiple is less than three.

Least affordable		Most affordable	
1	Ormskirk	1	Nelson
2	Carnforth	2	Bootle
3	Lytham St Annes	3	Leigh
4	Southport	4	Accrington
5	Prescot	5	Blackpool
6	Leyland	6	Newton le Willows
7	Chorley	7	Barrow-in-Furness
8	Bury	8	Blackburn
9	Warrington	9	Morecambe
10	Preston	10	Oldham

By district, Lancashire's most expensive place to buy property is the Ribble Valley. Average house prices here are more than twice as high as they are in the cheapest district, Burnley.

THE CO-OPERATIVE MOVEMENT AND ROCHDALE

The industrialisation of Lancashire during the 19th century changed workers' lives for the worse in many ways, but it also gave rise to a revolutionary new way of doing business – the co-operative movement.

Locally organised and jointly owned shops and mills had existed in Britain since the mid-1700s, but it wasn't until 28 weavers and other artisans got together in Rochdale in 1844 that the ideals and practices of co-operatives were properly established. When they opened a shop on Toad Lane to sell foodstuffs and a few other home goods, the Rochdale Equitable Pioneers Society also drew up a list of principles by which they would abide: of open membership and a fair voting system; and of putting any profits from their trading towards members' dividends – 'the divi' – and social projects like housing and education.

Although the project launched partly out of necessity – pitiful wages in towns like Rochdale having put even basic goods out of the reach of many – it was also inspired by a whole new take on trade, whereby workers would pull together to mutual benefit. The shop was instantly popular and prompted a spin-off mill to help supply it, and the group's template also inspired other groups to launch, around Lancashire, the country and the world. The Co-operative Union was formed in 1869, and by the end of the 19th century the country had more than 1,400 separate co-operative societies. These have merged over the years into large units offering a host of services from banking to travel to insurance as well as shopping, and the umbrella Co-operative Group now turns over about £10 billion a year, employs some 90,000 people and has around 2.5 million members. Throughout, it has remained admirably true to its principles of ethical trading, social responsibility and democratic decision-making – all derived from the eight original 'Rochdale Principles'.

The co-operative movement remains particularly strong in its home county, and Manchester is home to the Co-operative College. The Pioneers' original building on Toad Lane now houses the Rochdale Pioneers Museum, which has much more about the history of the co-operative movement and the town's role in its history (tel 01706 524920 or visit http://museum.co-op.ac.uk).

A MAP GLOSSARY

To the uninitiated, Ordnance Survey maps of Lancashire can be somewhat baffling. Filled with strange and wonderful words, many of which are unique to the county or northern England, they are an arcane introduction to the landscape. Here are 50 of the most common words and their meanings.

Barrow – small hill
Beck – mountain stream
Bield – shelter, usually for sheep but sometimes for humans
Breck – slope or hillside
Brook – small stream
Brow – summit of a hill or pass
Burn – small stream
Buttress – projecting part of a hill or mountain, usually a rock face
Cairn – pile of stones marking the top of a hill or the way up to it
Cam – crest of a hill
Carr – marsh or fen
Clough – steep-sided valley
Col – a flat, lower area, usually between two peaks
Combe or **coomb** – a hollow on the side of a hill
Common – open public land
Cove – sheltered recess in a hill
Crag – steep or rugged rock
Dale – valley
Dyke – either a watercourse or a bank or wall built to prevent flooding
Edge – either a narrow ridge or the outer slope of a range of hills
Fell – northern English term for hill
Fold – a hollow among hills
Force – waterfall
Gill or **ghyll** – small ravine or a stream that flows down it
Green – common grassy land
Gully – wide, steep cleft in a cliff
Heath – open, uncultivated land, often on sandy soil
Heights – rising ground
How – low hill
Intake – either a place where water is taken in to a channel or reclaimed land
Knoll – small hill or mound
Knott – craggy, rocky hill
Lea – pasture or meadowland

Man - cairn on a summit
Mere - lake or pond
Moor - open, undeveloped flatland
Moss - flat, marshy area
Nab - promontory of a hill
Pass - passage between mountains or valleys
Pike - sharp and rocky peaked hill or mountain
Rake - a pass through rocks
Ridge or **rigg** - long, narrow strip with steep drops on either side
Scar - bare, rocky outcrop
Side - vague term for something that has a dividing centre, like a hill
Sike or **syke** - small stream, often dry in summer
Slack - hollow area between two higher points, sometimes filled
  with water
Stile - either steps over a fence or wall or steep
Stone or **stones** - another word for cairn
Tarn - small mountain lake
Wash - sandbank exposed at low tide

LANCASHIRE FOOD – MORECAMBE BAY SHRIMPS AND COCKLES

Along more than 100 miles (161 km) of coastline, Lancashire has fished for shrimps and cockles for centuries. And around Morecambe Bay in particular – at 120 square miles (311 sq km) Britain's second largest bay after the Wash – they remain a popular local delicacy and export.

On the bay and further down the coast on the Irish Sea, shrimps are caught in nets that are trawled along the sands in shallow waters. Fishermen waded through the cold waters to cast them by hand at first, before employing horses and then tractors to pull them along. The Lancashire nobby, a distinctive trawler about 30 feet (9 m) in length and fast, agile and shallow enough to fish the low waters, became the craft of choice for fishermen from around the 1840s, and examples of them can sometimes still be seen today. Back on dry land, fishermen quickly boil up the shrimps and peel them – a fiddly job that used to be done by hand in homes but that is now more usually performed by machines in factories. After that, the shrimps are washed, packed or potted and perhaps frozen for transport.

If shrimping is a labour-intensive job, then cockling is back-breaking work. The cockles are buried a centimetre or so beneath the sands of Morecambe Bay, and become exposed once the tide recedes. They are then sucked to the surface using a 'jumbo' – essentially a plank of wood that softens the sand – and raked out. It is a tough enough job in fine weather, but when the wind and rain hammers across the bay it's one for only the hardiest of workers.

Both shrimps and cockles have a market among retailers and restaurants in Lancashire and neighbouring Cumbria, but a large proportion of sales are to Europe, where appreciation of them is far greater and they are used more creatively in cooking. The heavy demand means that cockles in particular can fetch good prices, and stocks have to be tightly controlled by stopping access if they have been over-farmed. On Morecambe Bay, shrimping and cockling are also subject to safety regulations, since the boggy sands and unpredictable, fast-moving tides make it a dangerous place to work. Restrictions were tightened after 23 Chinese immigrant workers drowned when they were overtaken by water while cockling on the bay in 2004, though there are concerns that inexperienced cocklers and shrimpers are still putting themselves at risk there.

A recipe for potted shrimps
250 g cooked Morecambe Bay shrimps
150 g butter
Good pinches of salt, cayenne pepper and nutmeg

Gently melt the butter. Stir in the shrimps and coat well. Add the salt, cayenne pepper and nutmeg and simmer on a low heat for five minutes, stirring often. Tip the mixture into pots and melt a little more butter in the hot pan to pour over the top of each pot to seal. Leave to cool and set. Serve either straight from the pot or gently warmed with brown bread or toast and a cup of tea for a snack, or mix the shrimps with other ingredients for a more substantial meal. They are particularly good tossed into pasta, stirred into a risotto or scattered over grilled or baked fish.

THE LANCASHIRE CUP WINNERS

The Lancashire Cup was a rugby league trophy contested by the county's leading clubs for more than 80 years. Alongside the Yorkshire Cup, it was formed after the great rugby schism of 1895 that separated the sport into the two codes of league and union, and soon became one of the most fiercely contested trophies among local rivals. Interrupted only by the two world wars, the Lancashire Cup was staged between

1905 and 1993, when leading clubs complained about the number of games they were having to play in all competitions and it was abandoned.

The 13 different clubs to have won the Lancashire Cup are:

Wigan (winners 21 times)

St Helens (11)

Warrington (9)

Oldham (8)

Widnes (7)

Salford (5)

Leigh (4)

Rochdale (4)

Swinton (4)

Barrow (2)

Broughton Rangers (2)

St Helens Recs (2)

Workington (1)

SOME PLACE NAMES AND THEIR MEANINGS: N TO Z

The origins of 60 more Lancashire place names.

Nelson – Takes its name from the Lord Nelson Inn, around which the town grew in the 19th century

Newbiggin – New building. Lancashire has several Newbiggins

Newton – New farmstead or village. Newton is another common Lancashire place name

Oldham – Old promontory. The town grew on the slopes of a sandstone ridge

Ormskirk – The church of Orm or similar name, Scandinavian in origin

Oswaldtwistle – Tongue of land in the fork of a river belonging to Oswald

Parbold – Building where pears grow

Peel Island – Takes its name from a peel castle built by the monks of Furness Abbey

Pendle – An Old English word for hill. Pendle Hill is therefore a tautology

Pennington - Farmstead paying a penny's rent

Plumpton - Farmstead where plum trees grow

Poulton - Farmstead or village by a pool. Lancashire has several Poultons

Prescot - Priests' cottage

Preston- Farmstead of the priests. Preston is a common English place name

Radcliffe - Red cliff

Ramsbottom - Probably the valley of the ram, though it could also refer to the valley where wild garlic grows

Rawtenstall - Farmstead on rough ground

Ribbleton - Farmstead or village on the River Ribble, which means rushing or tearing river

Ribchester - The Roman fort by the River Ribble

Rishton - Farmstead where rushes grow

Rochdale - Valley of the River Roch

Rossall - Nook or land where horses graze

Rossendale - Valley in the moor

Rusholme - Place at the rushes

St Annes - Takes its name from the 19th-century church of St Anne, the first building in the new town here

St Helens - Takes its name from a medieval chapel dedicated to St Helen

Salford - Ford by the willow trees

Samlesbury - Fortified place on a shelf of land

Sawrey - Muddy places

Scorton - Farmstead or village by a ravine or ditch

Sefton - Farmstead where rushes grow

Silverdale - Silver valley, probably from the grey limestone crags around the village

Skelmersdale - The valley of Skelmer or similar Scandinavian name

Southport - A modern town that was named in the late 18th century, possibly to position it in relation to ports further north in Lancashire

Stainton - Farmstead or village where there are stones

Standish - Stony pasture

Sutton - Farmstead or village in the south, in this case relative to St Helens. A common English place name

Swarthmoor - Black moor

Swinton - Farmstead where pigs are kept

Thornley - Clearing among or near thorns

Tottington - Farmstead of Totta or similar name

Trafford - Ford on a (Roman) road

Twiston - Farmstead or village at the fork of a river

Ulverston - Farmstead of Ulfr or similar Scandinavian name

Urswick – Farmstead or village by the bison lake

Vickerstown – A model town for workers in Barrow-in-Furness, built by the Vickers company

Walney Island – Island of quicksands

Walton – Farmstead or village of serfs. Walton is incorporated into several Lancashire place names

Warrington – Farmstead or village by a river dam

Warton – Look-out farmstead or village

Waterloo – Takes its name from Liverpool's Royal Waterloo Hotel, which in turn was named after the 1815 battle

Wavertree – Waving or swaying tree

Westhoughton – Farmstead in a nook of land. The west was added later to distinguish it from other Houghtons

Whalley – Woodland clearing near a round hill

Widnes – Wide promontory

Wigan – Probably derived from a longer Celtic name meaning Wigan's farmstead

Windermere – Takes its name from the adjacent lake, meaning the lake of Vinand or similar Scandinavian name

Woolton – Farmstead of Wulfa or similar name

Wrea Green – Corner or nook of land. Green was added later

Yealand – High land. Yealand is incorporated into several Lancashire place names

WRESTLING IN LANCASHIRE

From no-holds-barred violence to an Olympic sport – wrestling in Lancashire has come a long way, and it is still a respected part of the county's sporting tradition.

Organised wrestling dates back thousands of years, and its fans claim it as the oldest and purest sport known to man. Subtly diffe rent forms of it have endured all over the world, and English versions are still popular in areas of the north like the Lake District and Northumberland, where it was probably introduced by the Romans and later influenced by the Vikings. Many centuries later, Lancashire's wrestling advanced with the hugely popular traveling fairs or circuses, at which champion wrestlers would take on local challengers for money. Lancashire men began to be known as some of the toughest wrestlers going, a reputation that increased alongside the industry of coal mining. Grappling for fun or cash after long days in the pits, the county's best wrestlers were fearsomely strong, fit and wiry men.

Lancashire's wrestlers developed their own distinctive style, often called 'catch as catch can' or simply 'catch'. It involved players trying to catch hold of their opponent whichever way they could, using an array of ingenious and eye-watering grappling techniques. Victories were usually achieved via submission, when opponents conceded that they could take no more. While wrestling elsewhere started to introduce rules to minimise injuries, Lancashire's remained a much more primitive and violent sport, with bans on such alarming practices as eye gouging and choking only gradually introduced after overcoming protests from wrestling traditionalists.

'A Lancashire wrestling match is an ugly sight,' wrote one late 19th-century observer of the sport. 'The fierce animal passions of the men which mark the struggles of maddened bulls or wild beasts, the savage yelling of their partisans and the wrangling… are simply appalling.' Such criticism belied the dexterity, fitness and technique required to succeed, but there is little doubt that it was one of the most savage of organised sports. Lancashire's catch wrestling has, thankfully, evolved considerably since then. It is known more widely now as freestyle wrestling, an Olympic event that allows participants freedom of technique but with rules and time limits in place to stop things getting too painful.

The rising popularity of TV wrestling from both Britain and America, full of showmanship, glitz and staged manoeuvres, has drawn many young people away from the more traditional forms of the sport, but a handful of dedicated wrestling clubs remain in Lancashire, promoting it as a fun, friendly pastime for youngsters that improves strength, agility and confidence. Perhaps the most famous surviving club is Aspull Olympic in Wigan, set up by legendary Lancashire wrestler Billy Riley in the 1940s and once known rather ominously as 'the snakepit'. Bolton and Manchester also have centres that welcome newcomers.

ENGLISH HERITAGE PROPERTIES IN LANCASHIRE

English Heritage looks after seven properties in Lancashire, including some of the most important ruins of religious properties in the county. All open to the public, they are:

Furness Abbey, near Barrow-in-Furness

Sizeable sandstone ruins of an abbey founded in 1123 and at one time among the largest and most powerful in the country. Nearby is

Bow Bridge, a 15th-century stone bridge on a packhorse route to the abbey, also owned by English Heritage.

Goodshaw Chapel, near Rawtenstall
An interesting Baptist chapel built in 1760, with many original fittings and furnishings.

Piel Castle, near Barrow-in-Furness
Ruins of a 14th-century castle perched on Piel Island, built to defend Barrow against raiders. Visible from the mainland and accessible via a local ferry service, dependent on tides.

Sawley Abbey, near Clitheroe
A ruined 12th-century Cistercian abbey that was abandoned in the Dissolution. Dramatically located on the River Ribble.

Stott Park Bobbin Mill, near Newby Bridge
Former workers lead tours of this mill, opened in 1835 to produce the bobbins that kept Lancashire's spinning and weaving industries moving.

Warton Old Rectory
Upstanding ruins of a medieval limestone house, with the great hall particularly well preserved.

Whalley Abbey Gatehouse
A 14th-century gatehouse to a Cistercian abbey beside the River Calder.

TEN LONG DISTANCE WALKS

Lancashire has some 3,700 miles (5,955 km) of public rights of way – enough to stretch the entire length of Britain more than four times. The county's countryside offers many great walks, including some of Britain's most popular long distance trails. Here are ten waymarked routes, long and short, that are either entirely within Lancashire's boundaries or just pass through.

Brontë Way. Although the Brontë sisters are more commonly associated with Yorkshire, this 44-mile (71 km) route also takes in many of their Lancashire locations, including the starting point of Gawthorpe

Hall, where Charlotte often stayed, and Wycoller Hall, the inspiration for Ferndean Manor in her novel *Jane Eyre*. Across in Yorkshire, it takes in the sisters' birthplace, house and other inspirations.

Cumbria Coastal Way. Despite its name, this 150-mile (242 km) route takes in a large slice of 'proper' Lancashire's coastline, starting in Silverdale and passing around Morecambe Bay before leaving the county near Broughton-in-Furness. The way continues up to Gretna on the Scottish border.

Lancashire Coastal Way. Traces the county's coastline from Freckleton on the Ribble Estuary past Lytham St Annes, Blackpool and the Fylde coast, diverting inland to Lancaster then out again to Morecambe. The 137-mile (221 km) route ends at Silverdale where the Cumbria Coastal Way takes over (see above) – though Lancashire itself continues.

Lancashire Trail. A 70-mile (113 km) amble through some of the county's industrial and rural aspects, starting at St Helens and finishing at Thornton-le-Craven on the Yorkshire border.

Lancaster Canal. The towpath along the canal provides an easy to follow trail though north Lancashire, stretching 57 miles (92 km) from near Preston to Kendal in the Lake District.

Lune Valley Ramble. A pleasant lowland walk across north Lancashire, from Lancaster to Kirkby Lonsdale. At 17 miles (27 km), it can be done in a long day's walking.

Pendle Way. A 45-mile (72 km) circular trail starting and finishing at the Pendle Heritage Centre at Barrowford, and taking in the area made famous by Quaker George Fox and the Pendle Witches controversy. Follow the witch and broomstick logos on the signposts.

Ribble Way. Lovely 70-mile (113 km) walk tracing the route of the River Ribble, starting at its mouth near Preston and following its winding route past Clitheroe and other towns and villages up to its source, over the border at Yorkshire's Ribblehead.

Rossendale Way. A 45-mile (72 km) circular walk starting and finishing in Sharneyford, and taking in much of Rossendale's industrial heritage and old mill towns as well as its countryside.

Trans Pennine Trail. An alternative cross-country route, starting in Merseyside and mixing rural and urban trails as it passes Manchester before leaving the county for Yorkshire. The distance varies according to the spurs of the trail taken.

⬧⬧⬧⬧⬧⬧⬧⬧⬧⬧⬧⬧⬧⬧⬧⬧⬧⬧⬧⬧⬧⬧⬧⬧⬧⬧⬧⬧

SPORTSPEOPLE FROM LANCASHIRE

Lancashire has produced hundreds of outstanding sportspeople over the years, including dozens of football, cricket and rugby internationals and Olympic athletes. Here is a selection of 30 of them and their birthplaces.

Jimmy Armfield (Blackpool)
Michael Atherton (Manchester)
Bill Beaumont (Preston)
June Croft (Wigan)
William Webb Ellis (Salford)
Tom Finney (Preston)
Andrew Flintoff (Preston)
Carl Fogarty (Blackburn)
Bill Foulkes (St Helens)
Steven Gerrard (Whiston)
Ron Greenwood (Worsthorne)
Reg Harris (Bury)
Ron Hill (Accrington)
Emlyn Hughes (Barrow-in-Furness)
Geoff Hurst (Ashton-under-Lyne)
Amir Khan (Bolton)
Nat Lofthouse (Bolton)
David Lloyd (Accrington)
Mary Peters (Halewood)
Jason Queally (Chorley)
Wayne Rooney (Liverpool)
Nigel Short (Leigh)
Tommy Smith (Liverpool)
Brian Statham (Manchester)
Nobby Stiles (Manchester)
Frank Swift (Blackpool)
Phil Thompson (Liverpool)
Ernest Tyldesley (Worsley)
Frank Tyson (Bolton)
Cyril Washbrook (Clitheroe)

※※※※※※※※※※※※※※※※※※※※※※※

SOME LANCASHIRE CITIES AND TOWNS AROUND THE WORLD

As the Empire and British people spread around the world, some familiar Lancashire place names began to appear in far-flung corners of the world. America, Australia, New Zealand and other Commonwealth countries all have a sprinkling of villages, towns and counties named after Lancashire; here are some of the most interesting locations.

Blackburn
Hastings, New Zealand
KwaZulu-Natal, South Africa
Missouri, US
Oklahoma, US

Bolton
Victoria, Australia
Ontario, Canada
Saint Ann, Jamaica
Davao del Sur, Philippines
Massachusetts, US
Mississippi, US
North Carolina, US
Harare, Zimbabwe

Burnley
Victoria, Australia
Eastern Cape, South Africa

Lancaster
Victoria, Australia
Saint James, Barbados
Ontario, Canada
Upper Demerara-Berbice,
   Guyana
Trelawny, Jamaica
California, US
Kentucky, US
Nebraska, US
Pennsylvania, US
South Carolina, US
Texas, US
Bulawayo, Zimbabwe

Leigh
New South Wales,
   Australia
Auckland, New Zealand
Nebraska, US

Liverpool
New South Wales,
   Australia
Nova Scotia, Canada
Illinois, US
New York, US
Pennsylvania, US
Texas, US

Manchester
South Jamaica
Georgia, US
Iowa, US
Kentucky, US
Missouri, US
New Hampshire, US
Tennessee, US
Washington, US

Preston
Victoria, Australia
Ontario, Canada
Georgia, US
Idaho, US
Iowa, US
Maryland, US
Minnesota, US
West Virginia, US

Southport	**Warrington**
Queensland, Australia	Kilkenny, Ireland
Newfoundland, Canada	Dunedin, New Zealand
KwaZulu-Natal, South Africa	Florida, US
New York, US	
North Carolina, US	

LANCASHIRE ON SCREEN – BROOKSIDE

If *Coronation Street* has always been Lancashire's top TV show then *Brookside*, throughout the 1980s and much of the 1990s, was its second favourite – an edgy young upstart to the comfortable familiarity of the long-running soap opera.

The programme was created for Channel 4 and was first broadcast on the station's opening night in November 1982. It was designed by creator Phil Redmond as Liverpool's answer to Manchester's *Corrie* – a story of life in the modern city suburbs rather than Lancashire's old terraces. At a time when competition for ratings among the various channels' soaps was fierce, *Brookside* soon tried to distinguish itself with a reputation for topical, controversial and taboo storylines. That led it to tackle some serious issues, at times handled with sensitivity and typical Liverpudlian humour. Over time, though, it led the show into more convoluted and outlandish plots, and prompted in particular a death rate that exceeded even the sky-high ones of *Coronation Street* and Yorkshire's *Emmerdale*. Over 2,915 episodes, *Brookside* killed off a total of 74 characters and sundry pets via ingenious and increasingly gruesome means including murders, suicides, drug overdoses, car accidents, gas explosions, firebombs and helicopter crashes.

There were plenty of births and weddings too, but *Brookside* became known as a somewhat depressing and violent soap opera as well as a socially aware one. From a peak of around 8 million viewers and three episodes a week in the early 1990s, ratings had tumbled to fewer than a million and a single weekend show by the end of the decade, thanks to a combination of the outlandish plots, unpopular characters, poor scheduling and competition from other soaps and programmes. It struggled on to its 21st anniversary in 2003 but was pulled soon afterwards, its residents moved out to make way for a waste incinerator. Tucked away in a late-night TV slot, the show went out in a blaze of swearing, a lynching of a local drug dealer and a knowing script that saw the last man out daub a 'd' on the street sign to read 'Brookside Closed'.

Brookside got much of its realism from the custom-built set on which it was filmed – a cul-de-sac of houses in the West Derby suburb of Liverpool. Some of the houses were used for other TV productions after the soap ended, though they were later sold off to property developers. That, however, has not stopped intermittent campaigns for the show to be revived.

ENGELS IN LANCASHIRE

Although they were not generally noted for their reformist tendencies, a handful of men among Lancashire's generation of mill owners did at least attempt to temper their pursuit of vast wealth with sympathies for the people who toiled for them. And nowhere was the dichotomy more striking than in Friedrich Engels, whose years in Lancashire were to shape his hugely influential thinking and writing.

Engels travelled to Manchester from Germany in his early twenties, dispatched by his mill owner father to look after the family's interests in the town. The intention was to distract Engels from his radical politics, but the move only advanced his communist doctrines by making him aware of the dreadful living and working conditions of the men, women and children who slaved in Manchester's mills. During the working day Engels looked after the family business, but at other times he explored Manchester's appalling slums, gathering material for what was to become his classic social document: *The Condition of the Working Class in England*. 'Everywhere are half or wholly ruined buildings,' he wrote. 'Everywhere heaps of debris, refuse and offal; standing pools and gutters; and a stench which alone would make it impossible for a human being in any degree civilised to live in such a district.' The book was not translated into English for more than 40 years, though Engels' sympathies for the working class and contempt for the exploitative bourgeoisie of Lancashire and beyond had already excited fellow radicals by then.

Engels' experiences in Manchester also helped to bolster his association with Karl Marx, and they published their landmark *Manifesto of the Communist Party* together in 1848. Engels returned to Manchester after several years in various European cities, and worked again in the family business to fund his and Marx's campaigns. The irony that he was trying to advance the cause of the working classes while running one of the very businesses that kept them in poverty was not lost on him. Engels later moved to London to be nearer Marx, and died there in 1895.

ROSES RECORDS

No fixtures in England's county cricket are more fiercely contested than those between Lancashire and Yorkshire. The white rose county won the inaugural first-class Roses match between the two sides in 1849 and, to Lancastrians' great frustration, have held the upper hand ever since, with substantially more wins and the vast majority of the fixture's team and individual records. Here are the leading achievements from a century and a half of cross-Pennine competition, correct to the start of the 2010 season.

261 . . . . total first-class Roses fixtures played

52 . . . . matches won by Lancashire

80 . . . . matches won by Yorkshire

129 . . . . matches drawn

3,006 . . . . most runs in Roses matches, by Herbert Sutcliffe (Yorkshire)

590 . . . . highest team score, by Yorkshire in 1887

252 . . . . highest individual score, by Darren Lehmann (Yorkshire) in 2001

10 . . . . most centuries in Roses matches, by Geoff Boycott (Yorkshire)

237 . . . . most wickets in Roses matches, by Wilfred Rhodes (Yorkshire)

9 for 23 . . . . best bowling in an innings, by George Hirst (Yorkshire) in 1910

17 for 91 . . . . . best bowling in a match, by Harry Dean (Lancashire) in 1913

101 . . . . most wicket-keeping victims in Roses matches, by David Bairstow (Yorkshire)

65 . . . . most catches in Roses matches by a fielder, by John Tunnicliffe (Yorkshire)

THE CELEBRITIES OF BLACKPOOL'S ILLUMINATIONS

Since Lord Derby first did the honours in 1934, the switching-on of the Blackpool Illuminations has been a big annual event in the town. And as the reputation of the spectacular display of lights spread over the years, so the town began to attract some popular celebrities, both local and international, to flick the switch each summer. The roll call of celebs takes in actors, TV and radio stars, sportspeople and even a famous racecourse and puppets. Here are 20 of the best known names to have turned on the lights since the Second World War.

Stanley Matthews (1951)

George Formby (1953)

Jayne Mansfield (1959)

Gracie Fields (1964)

Ken Dodd (1966)

Matt Busby (1968)

The cast of Dad's Army (1971)

Gordon Banks (1973)

Red Rum (1977)

Kermit the Frog and the Muppets (1979)

The cast of *Coronation Street* (1983)

Les Dawson (1986)

Frank Bruno (1989)

Shirley Bassey (1994)

The Bee Gees (1995)

Gary Barlow (1999)

Ronan Keating (2002)

Geri Halliwell (2004)

Chris Evans (2005)

David Tennant (2007)

GREAT LANCASTRIANS –
ANDREW FLINTOFF

Several Lancastrians have achieved more in sporting terms, but few have embodied the county's virtues of gutsy determination and hard but fair play quite so well as cricketer Andrew Flintoff.

Flintoff was born in Preston in 1977 and played his early cricket on the Lancashire coast for St Annes, where new tiles on the roofs of several houses around the club's ground are evidence of his thunderous shots. Progressing to Lancashire's county team at 17, he moved through England's youth ranks and into the Test side for the first time in 1997. He soon became known as a powerful all-rounder – an aggressive hitter, intimidating fast bowler and reliable fielder – but his early performances for his country were mixed.

It wasn't until 2005 that Flintoff established himself as England's best and best-loved cricketer since Ian Botham. In a tense and thrilling series against Australia, Flintoff's batting, bowling and sheer will to win helped England to win the Ashes for the first time in 18 years. Revered by fans and respected and feared by opponents, over the course of one glorious summer he became a cricketing superstar.

Like all good folk heroes, Flintoff's career has not been without its blemishes. He admitted to being overweight in his early playing days, and he has run into occasional drink-related controversies, celebrating the 2005 Ashes in somewhat enthusiastic style and drowning his sorrows on England's disastrous tour of Australia in 2006-7 as he captained the side to a 5-0 defeat. He has always been susceptible to injuries, and after a succession of setbacks and rehabilitations, he announced his intention to retire from Test match cricket after the 2009 series against Australia. Typically, he went on to make crucial contributions in a final hurrah as England regained the Ashes once more.

Flintoff's honours have included an MBE, the BBC's Sports Personality of the Year award – of which he remains, with Mary Peters, one of only two Lancashire-born winners – and, not least, the freedom of his home city of Preston. His final Test match averages of 32 with the bat and 33 with the ball are a little way off the benchmarks for top players, but they do not reveal his talismanic qualities nor his ability to conjure up great performances at the most important times. Through all the ups and downs he has remained loyal to Lancashire and true to its values – and his highest ever score remains the 232 not out he clobbered for St Annes as a 14-year-old.

THE ROYAL LANCASHIRE SHOW

Agricultural shows have long been a way for rural Lancashire to get together and celebrate its achievements, and for more than two centuries the Royal Lancashire Show has been the most important date in the calendar.

The show claims to be able to trace its roots back to 1767, making it one of the oldest shows of its kind in the country. For most of its history it has rotated through venues across Lancashire, befo re settling for many years in Blackpool's Stanley Park. Over three days each July, the show celebrated the achievements of farmers, breeders and others, mixing agricultural and lifestock competition with family entertainment. Dozens of animal classes would draw hundreds of entries from the northwest and beyond, while thousands of visitors enjoyed countryside crafts, equestrian events, exhibitions and food and beer tents.

But while the show's history is long and proud, the last few decades of it have been less glorious. Financial problems led its parent company to cancel the show for several years in the late 1970s, before it was reconvened at various venues including Blackburn, Chorley and Ribchester. Traffic issues, disagreements with local councils and landownersand criticisms that the show had lost touch with its farming roots all increased the problems, which were capped off when terrible weather forced organisers to cancel the show at short notice in both 2007 and 2008. The huge financial losses incurred as a result have led to subsequent events being pulled too, though if a new venue and sponsors can be found it may be revived in the future.

LANCASTRIANS IN FOOTBALL'S HALL OF FAME

Of the 70 or so men in football's hall of fame, a good proportion – eleven – were born in Lancashire. That is very appropriate, as the hall of fame was created at the National Football Museum in Preston, the Lancastrian city often regarded as the cradle if not the exact birthplace of the game.

Members of the hall of fame are chosen by a panel of experts, and sometimes by a public vote. To qualify, players must be aged over 30 and have played in England for at least five years. With a goalkeeper, a couple of defenders and midfielders and five renowned strikers among them, Lancashire's eleven Hall of Famers make for a formidable and attack-minded line-up. The eleven, together with their places of birth, are:

Jimmy Armfield (Denton)

Alan Ball (Farnworth)

Tom Finney (Preston)

Emlyn Hughes (Barrow-in-Furness)

Roger Hunt (Golborne)

Geoff Hurst (Ashton-under-Lyne)

Tommy Lawton (Farnworth)

Nat Lofthouse (Bolton)

Paul Scholes (Salford)

Nobby Stiles (Manchester)

Frank Swift (Blackpool)

Two more Lancastrians – Ron Greenwood (born in Worstorne), and Walter Winterbottom (Oldham), are featured in the managers' section of the football hall of fame. Two sides from the county – the Manchester United team of 1968 and Liverpool's of 1978 – are also included.

ᏣᏅᏣᏋᏣᏅᏣᏋᏣᏅᏣᏋᏣᏅᏣᏋᏣᏅᏣᏋᏣᏅᏣᏋᏣᏅᏣᏋᏣᏅᏣᏋᏣᏅᏣᏋ

THE RISE, FALL AND RISE OF THE TRAM

At their peak they criss-crossed Lancashire, and at their lowest point they were all but obliterated. Now, more than a century after they first ran, tramways are again becoming an integral part of the county's transport infrastructure.

Trams have carried the British public since Swansea opened the world's first passenger-carrying line in 1807. But their golden era can be traced to Blackpool, which created the country's inaugural electric street line when it opened in 1885. It was an instant hit with locals and holidaymakers, and was soon extended to the Pleasure Beach in one direction and Fleetwood in the other, eventually spanning more than 11 miles (18 km) and 61 stops. Inspired by Blackpool's success, other towns put up their own tramways. Accrington, Blackburn, Bolton, Burnley, Lancaster, Liverpool, Morecambe, Preston, Rochdale, St Helens and Wigan – all these places and many more at one time had large or small systems of their own, at first pulled by horses and then powered by electricity or, sometimes, by steam. At its peak the network was so large that passengers could traverse much of the county via interlinking services.

Much as the railways had expanded far beyond the market for them, so it soon became apparent that many of the tramways could not pay their way. They fell out of favour as the 20th century wore on, shunted off the roads by the increasing number of cars. Many of the smaller towns' tram companies folded in the 1930s, though networks survived in Manchester and Liverpool until 1949 and 1957 respectively. From that first wave of tram building in the 19th century, Blackpool's is the only urban line to survive today.

But whereas trams' dominance of the road was once seen as an inconvenience, now it is heralded an advantage and an opportunity to get motorists out of their cars and into environmentally friendlier public transport. Manchester became the first city to restore trams to the streets when it opened its Metrolink network in 1992, and it was soon followed by others including Sheffield and Birmingham. It now carries around 20 million people a year and has invested heavily in an expansion that will bring its number of stops to around 100. Blackpool has recently poured £100m into new vehicles and line improvements for the 7 million passengers it serves annually. And more than half a century after it closed, Liverpool has plans for a brand new tramway of its own, though these have already been much delayed.

The best place to find out more about the history of trams in Lancashire is the Museum of Transport in Manchester, which holds a large collection of restored vehicles (tel 0161 205 2122 or visit www.gmts.co.uk).

LANCASHIRE'S UNUSUAL WORLD RECORD HOLDERS

Lancashire has more than its fair share of sporting, cultural and scientific high achievers, but it has plenty of record holders in less distinguished disciplines, too. Here are ten of the strangest – and perhaps most pointless – world records set in the county, all verified by Guinness.

Largest cup of tea

Measuring 4 feet (1.22 m) in diameter and height, and with a volume of 400 litres, this was made as a publicity stunt by Lancashire Tea at Asda's Preston store in 2008.

Longest convoy of limousines

Blackpool's Golden Mile was the appropriate setting for this world record, which saw well over 100 stretch limousines from all over the country drive in convoy in 2008. Money was raised for charity from passengers paying to be part of the record.

Biggest Christmas Pudding

At the most recent Aughton Pudding Feast in 1992, the village turned out a Christmas Pudding that weighed in at around 3.3 tons. It took a week to produce and required an industrial concrete mixer to stir up its ingredients.

Highest stack of poppadoms

Achieved by the staff of the Indian Ocean Restaurant in Ashton-under-Lyne in 2007, when they built a pile 4.85 feet (1.48 m) high.

Biggest pancake

Another food record – this one set in Rochdale in 1994 with a 3-ton, 49-feet (15 m) diameter pancake.

Most netball goals scored in one hour

257 – set by local players in Manchester's Piccadilly Gardens in 2009.

Longest rollercoaster ride

Another Blackpool record – this time achieved by New Yorker Richard Rodriguez who rode the Big One at Blackpool Pleasure Beach for 401 hours in July and August 2007. He completed nearly 8,000 rides and covered around 6,300 miles (10,139 km).

Fastest window cleaner

The record for the fastest cleaning of three windows – 9.14 seconds by Terry Burrows – was set in Blackpool in 2009.

Most car tyres balanced on head

Ten – achieved by John Evans at the Burnley Balloon Festival in 2008.

Biggest Hot Pot

Made at Garstang in 2007, this weighed in at 209 kg and used 35 kg of Bowland lamb, 35 kg of onions and 100 kg of potatoes. Given that this is Lancashire's leading dish, it will be an embarrassment to the county if the record is ever beaten anywhere else.

LANCASHIRE'S DOZEN CRICKET GROUNDS

Lancashire County Cricket Club has played first-class fixtures at a dozen different grounds up and down the county since its first match in 1865. As attendances dwindled from the club's heyday and the cost of putting on games outside of the club's headquarters rose, so the number of venues has declined over the years. Two popular outposts – Southport and Lytham St Annes – were dropped from the first-class fixture list in the late 1990s, and nowadays only three – in Manchester, Liverpool and Blackpool – are in active use, but the list of former grounds is a nostalgic reminder of how Lancashire's cricketers were once revered across the county. Together with the year in which first-class games were last hosted there, Lancashire's dozen grounds are:

Wavertree Road, Liverpool (1866)
Station Road, Whalley (1867)
Castleton, Rochdale (1876)
Lune Road, Lancaster (1914)
Alexandra Meadows, Blackburn (1935)
Seed Hill, Nelson (1938)
West Cliff, Preston (1952)
Church Road, Lytham St Annes (1998)
Trafalgar Road, Southport (1999)
Aigburth, Liverpool (to present)
Old Trafford, Manchester (to present)
Stanley Park, Blackpool (to present)

LANCASHIRE INDUSTRY – AEROSPACE

The decline of cotton, coal and other industries has hit Lancashire hard over the years, but the county remains one of Britain's great manufacturing powerhouses. Even though numbers are perhaps a third of what they were at their peak before and after the First World War, around 100,000 workers are still employed in manufacturing here – equivalent to one in six of Lancashire's total workforce, compared to just one in nine nationwide. And nearly a quarter of those manufacturing employees rely for their work on the aerospace industry.

Lancashire's role in the industry goes back more than a century, to the earliest days of flight. In 1909, many of the country's pioneering aviators demonstrated their skills at the Blackpool Aviation Week, Britain's first ever air show. A year earlier, Salford-born Alliott Verdon Roe had become the first Englishman to complete a powered flight, and in 1910 he launched the world's first manufacturing firm dedicated solely to aircraft. His company, later abbreviated to Avro, lasted until the 1960s and was responsible for numerous landmark aircraft like the Lancaster and Vulcan Bombers along the way.

Roe's firm and the others in Lancashire that soon followed it were among the few to benefit from the First World War, turning out several thousand aircraft for the government. Afterwards, the industry refined its aircraft and developed innovations like flying boats, many of them produced by the newly formed English Electric Company at Preston, which also helped build the country's rail and tram networks. But it was the government's rearmament programme ahead of the Second World War that sent Lancashire's industry into overdrive. Because the textile and other industries had established a strong engineering and labour base in the county, and because it was less likely than southern centres to face German bombing, Lancashire was perfectly placed to meet the rush of aircraft orders. In the early 1940s, some 50,000 people across the county worked flat out to support the war effort, turning out around 30,000 aircraft in the decade or so before, during and after the hostilities – nearly one in four of Britain's total planes in that time.

Lancashire's manufacturing capacity inevitably declined after the war, but it adjusted well to new demands by designing and producing civilian aircraft and an increasingly sophisticated range of jet fighters. Nowadays it remains a highly skilled and internationally respected centre of excellence for the air, space and defence industries, responsible for perhaps a fifth of the UK's aerospace output. The county's order book also includes projects for governments and air companies across the world, and production has brought with it plenty of spin-off industries and sub-contractors – for engines, parts, missiles, ground support equipment, testing and, at Barrow-in-Furness in particular, airships. Well over 100 companies in Lancashire are now directly or indirectly linked to aircraft and defence manufacture, including giants like BAE Systems in Preston, Aircelle in Burnley and Rolls Royce in Barnoldswick as well as dozens of highly specialised smaller firms. In all, Lancashire has probably produced at least 50,000 civilian and military aircraft since 1910, as well as important elements for tens of thousands more.

THE LANCASHIRE OPERA

Lancashire has much modern music of which it can be proud – but not too many operas. The most famous to be connected to the county is *Emilia di Liverpool*, written by the prolific Italian composer Gaetano Donizetti at the age of 27, though based on an existing libretto, and premiered in Naples in 1824.

Liverpool owes its role in the opera to a Romantic fascination with Britain on the continent, and its importance as a port would have meant it was fairly well known in Italy at the time as a glamorous, far-off place. The opera, partly serious but with plenty of humour, relates the story of Emilia, courted and then deserted by a suitor, and the consequent emotional turmoil including the death of her ashamed mother before things are tied up in a satisfactorily happy ending.

The opera was not a critical success, and despite several reworkings by Donizetti, it soon fell into obscurity. It has been revived twice in Liverpool – in 1957 to help mark the 750th anniversary of the city's royal charter, and again in 2008 as part of its programme as the European Capital of Culture. *Emilia*'s popularity among audiences on both occasions was not diminished by its somewhat sketchy impressions of Liverpool, which placed the town among forests and mountains not far north of London.

LANCASHIRE POEMS –
'GOD HELP THE POOR'

Samuel Bamford was one of the most radical of all Lancashire poets. He was born in 1788 in Middleton, near Oldham and Rochdale, and, like many of his contemporaries, started work as a weaver before discovering poetry. He sympathised with the downtrodden working classes and became even angrier at their treatment after Manchester's 'Peterloo Massacre' of 1819, when the government's forces broke up a peaceful gathering of workers campaigning for reform and universal suffrage, killing at least 15. Bamford, who had led a march to the site of the massacre, was imprisoned for a year. On his release, he wrote widely on the tribulations of the working classes and, after a spell of employment in London, returned to Lancashire and the job of weaving. His forthright, radical views alienated some, but his popularity was such that thousands turned out for his funeral in 1872.

Bamford was especially good at chronicling the experiences of Lancashire weavers and other workers who had seen their old ways of life overturned by the Industrial Revolution. This extract from 'God Help The Poor' is typical of his heartfelt if somewhat sentimental radicalism.

God help the poor, who on this wintry morn
Come forth of alleys dim, and courts obscure!
God help yon poor pale girl, who droops forlorn,
And meekly her affliction doth endure!
God help the outcast lamb! She trembling stands,
All wan her lips, and frozen rod her hands;
Her mournful eyes are modestly down cast,
Her night-black hair streams on the fitful blast;
Her bosom, passing fair, is half reveal'd,
And, oh! so cold, the snow lies there congeal'd;
Her feet benumb'd, her shoes all rent and worn:
God help thee, outcast lamb, who stand'st forlorn! God help the poor!

God help the poor! Another have I found,
A bow'd and venerable man is he;
His slouched hat with faded crape is bound;
His coat is grey, and thread-bare too, I see,
The rude winds seem to mock his hoary hair;
His shirtless bosom to the blast is bare.
Anon he turns, and casts a wistful eye,
And with scant napkin wipes the blinding spray;
And looks again, as if he fain would spy
Friends he hath feasted in his better day:
Ah! some are dead, and some have long forborne
To know the poor; and he is left forlorn! God help the poor!

God help the poor, who in lone valleys dwell,
Or by far hills, where whin and heather grow!
Theirs is a story sad indeed to tell;
Yet little cares the world, nor seeks to know
The toil and want poor weavers undergo.
The irksome loom must have them up at morn;
They work till worn-out nature will have sleep;
They taste, but are not fed. Cold snow drifts deep
Around the fireless cot, and blocks the door;
The night-storm howls a dirge o'er moss and moor.
And shall they perish thus, oppress'd and lorn?
Shall toil and famine hopeless, still be borne?
No! God will yet arise and help the poor!

THE MEANINGS OF LANCASHIRE'S RIVER, CANAL AND LAKE NAMES

Most of the rivers in Lancashire derive their names from Celtic words associated with water. Here are some of the major rivers and their meanings, together with a few of Lancashire's canals and lakes.

Asland – Ash tree river. It is also known as the Douglas, meaning black or dark river

Blakewater – Black river. It gives its name to Blackburn

Brathay – Broad river

Bridgewater Canal – From the Dukes of Bridgewater, who planned and funded the canal

Brun – Brown river. The town of Burnley takes its name from it

Calder – 'Hard' stream, probably meaning rocky in this context

Chor – Unusual in that the river takes its name from the town it flows through, rather than the other way round

Cocker and **Conder** – Crooked river

Coniston Water – Named after the village of Coniston, meaning king's settlement

Crake – Rocky river

Croal – Winding stream

Darwen – River where oak trees grow

Duddon – The origins of this river are uncertain, though it and the Duddon Valley could be named after a man called Dudda or similar

Esthwaite Water – Lake by the ash tree clearing

Greta – Stony stream

Hindburn – Hind's stream

Hodder – Might take its name from the Celtic for boundary; it is the traditional border between Lancashire and the West Riding of Yorkshire

Irk – Possibly derived from the word for roebuck, indicating a fast-running river

Irwell – Winding stream

Kent – Holy river

Leven – Smooth-flowing river

Lune – Pure, health-giving river

Martin Mere – Settlement by the lake

Mersey – Boundary river

Ribble – Rushing or tearing river

Roch - Takes its name from the word meaning place with a homestead or hall

Roddlesworth - Probably derived from the homestead of Hrothwulf or similar name

Roeburn - River of the female roe deer

Sankey Canal - Named after the valley of the Sankey Brook down which it runs

Tame - Probably dark river, though its origins, like those of the Thames and other similarly named rivers, are the subject of debate

Wenning - Dark river

Windermere - The lake of Vinand or similar Scandinavian name

Winster - River on the left

Wyre - Winding river

Yarrow - Rough river

GREAT LANCASTRIANS – WILLIAM LEVER

Rising from a grocer's apprentice to a global business tycoon, the story of William Lever is remarkable enough in business terms alone. But Lever is also remembered as a man who revolutionised Victorian workers' conditions and rights and – along perhaps with Henry Tate – as the greatest philanthropist in Lancashire's history.

Lever was born in 1851 in Bolton and, in common with many of Lancashire's great entrepreneurs, started work young, having left school at 15. Having joined his father's modest grocery business, he stumbled upon the simple product that was to make his fortune – soap. Previously manufactured in huge slabs from which smaller pieces were cut as and when they were needed, Lever's great idea was to package and sell individual bars to the public. His products – launched with the intention 'to make cleanliness commonplace; to lessen work for women; to foster health and contribute to personal attractiveness' – quite literally cleaned up Victorian Britain.

Lever's brands like Sunlight Soap were soon hugely popular, and having joined forces with his brother, James, he opened a factory in Warrington to make his own, higher quality soap. Lever Brothers grew rapidly, and by the early 19th century had taken its products into more than 100 countries worldwide, established its own palm oil plantation in Africa, and diversified into countless other products. Lever became, successively, a baronet, lord and viscount and, not least, High Sheriff of Lancashire and Mayor of Bolton. His name lives on in the vast consumer goods empire of Unilever, and at the turn of the millennium he was voted fourth in a BBC poll to find Britain's greatest ever business leader.

Perhaps remembering the squalid conditions of working class areas of Bolton, and inspired by strong religious beliefs, Lever's philanthropy became evident as soon as he started to make money. Having opened new soap factories on the Wirral, he created Port Sunlight – a brand new 'model' village for his workers with spacious housing and facilities like schools and libraries. Lever's companies' pay and conditions were better than average, too, and he campaigned for workers' rights after getting elected as an MP for the Wirral. He wasn't the only businessman of his generation to think in this altruistic way – and his complicit role in forced labour at his African plantation indicates that his philanthropy had limits – but he was among the first and most determined of those who put their ideals of greater social equality into practice.

Lever also had a lasting impact on the village of Rivington, where he lived for many years and opened a park, tower, zoo, replica of the ruined Liverpool Castle and several other buildings for the benefit of local citizens. In nearby Bolton he funded schools and churches, and bought for the town Hall i'th Wood, the manor house of Samuel Crompton. He also bought the island of Lewis and Harris in the western Scottish isles, where the town of Leverburgh is named after him, and set up the Leverhulme Trust, which continues as a research and education charity today.

LANCASHIRE FOOD – TRIPE

While traditional Lancashire delicacies like hot pot and black pudding have enjoyed something of a renaissance lately, tripe is a dish that, for younger generations at least, is largely consigned to history. Worse, it has become a cliché of unappealing food in northern England for those who have never been there. But before so many people became squeamish or patronising about it, cuts of offal like tripe were hugely popular across Lancashire as cheap, filling and nutritious alternatives to expensive prime fillets.

Tripe is the stomach lining of an animal – sometimes sheep, pigs or goats, but most often a cow. Beef tripe comes in several forms, depending on the chamber of the stomach from which it is taken, and can be flat or honeycombed in texture as a result. Lancashire once had hundreds of tripe shops and stalls specialising purely in this and other cheap cuts, serving mill and factory workers in the industrial towns and, in wartime, helping people overcome meat rationing.

Changing tastes and bad memories associated with poorly cooked tripe mean these retailers have all but died out now, and these days you are much more likely to find it on the menus of restaurants in Italy or France than in Lancashire.

Good butchers, though, should still be able to sell you tripe, and they and its producers have tried to increase its appeal, by thoroughly cleaning and boiling it before sale to remove unpleasant odours, and treating it in citric solutions to bleach the colour white from its natural sludgy brown. Even after that, tripe requires another good cleaning before cooking, and prolonged boiling to soften it for eating. It is sometimes served simply with salt and vinegar or incorporated into stews or casseroles, but the classic Lancashire way has always been to pair it with lashings of onions in a creamy sauce.

A recipe for tripe and onions

500 g tripe, thoroughly washed and cleaned
3 medium onions
30 g butter
2 tbsp plain flour
1 tsp mustard
600 ml chicken stock
40 ml double cream
Salt and freshly ground black pepper

Cut the tripe into large pieces about 2 inches (5 cm) across, and thickly slice the onions. Melt the butter in a large pan and fry the onions over a low heat until softened. Add the flour and mustard and stir well, and then add the tripe pieces. After stirring again, pour in the stock, season with salt and pepper and boil for between one and two hours, or until the tripe is tender – cooking times can vary widely. Keep an eye on the consistency of the sauce towards the end of the cooking time, adding a little more stock or water if it's too thick and letting a little out if it's too thin. Just before serving, pour in the double cream and season again if required. Serve with mashed potato.

TEN LANCASHIRE BOOKS

Lancashire's towns, cities and countryside have inspired hundreds of writers over the centuries. From all-time classics to romantic sagas to contemporary literary fiction, this is a selection of ten books set in the county.

The Lancashire Witches by William Harrison Ainsworth
An undervalued Victorian novel that blends the Gothic supernatural,
romance and the political context of the Pendle witch hunts.

A Kind of Loving by Stan Barstow
Lancashire town life forms the backdrop to a melancholy romance
in this popular novel of the 1960s. It was turned into a film a
couple of years after it was published and, along with its sequels,
into a TV series in the 1980s. It is often bracketed in the social
realist or 'kitchen sink' genres of fiction and drama.

Hard Times by Charles Dickens
The town of Coketown in which this classic novel of industrial
misery is set is fictional, but it was firmly inspired by Dickens'
visit to Preston in 1854 and his concern for the welfare of the men,
women and children living and working there.

North and South by Elizabeth Gaskell
A classic novel contrasting the poor industrial urban north of
the working classes with the more affluent rural south. The
northern town is called Milton in the novel, but is closely based
on Manchester, where Gaskell lived for a while. The book was
recently adapted for a popular BBC TV series. Gaskell's Mary
Barton was also set in Manchester.

Love on the Dole by Walter Greenwood
Written in the early 1930s and set during a period of economic
crisis in a poverty-stricken area of Salford where Greenwood
grew up, this novel tells of the effects of unemployment on a
single family. It was acclaimed for highlighting both the deprivation
in northern England and the stoicism with which it was tackled,
and was later adapted into a film, play and TV series.

Farewell to Lancashire by Anna Jacobs
Just one of the many historical and romantic sagas set in the
county by this prolific author. This one is told against the backdrop
of Lancashire's 'cotton famine' when the American Civil War hit
the import of cotton into the county's mills.

The Road to Wigan Pier by George Orwell
Classic documentary of life in economically depressed Lancashire
and other parts of northern England, published a few years before
the Second World War. Orwell spent time in Wigan and nearby
coal mines to research the book. He intended his title to be ironic,

though the area around part of the canal running through the town is now known as Wigan Pier.

The Tales of Peter Rabbit by Beatrix Potter
Most of Potter's books for children were inspired by the creatures, people and places of the area around her home of Hill Top at Near Sawrey, just inside Lancashire's borders in the far north of the county.

Mr Wroe's Virgins by Jane Rogers
The story of seven female disciples of John Wroe, a prophet of an apocalyptic church with its headquarters in Lancashire in the 1820s.

Oranges Are Not the Only Fruit by Jeanette Winterson
Born in Manchester and brought up in Accrington in a heavily religious family, Winterson's book is partly the story of her own complicated Lancashire childhood.

THE SEVEN WONDERS OF LANCASHIRE

As chosen by the county's leading magazine, *Lancashire Life*.

Liverpool Anglican Cathedral
Manchester Town Hall
Pendle Hill
St Walburge's Church, Preston
Blackpool Tower
The Ashton Memorial, Lancaster
The Old Man of Coniston

ACKNOWLEDGEMENTS

I am indebted to numerous organisations and individuals for providing information, ideas and advice during the writing of this book. I am grateful in particular to the staff, publications and websites of the following: the Astley Green Colliery Museum; the Battlefields Trust; the Beatles Story; the Bolton, Bowland Pennine, Coniston, Kendal and Rossendale and Pendle mountain rescue teams; the Department for Environment, Food and Rural Affairs; the Dry Stone Walling Association; English Heritage; the English Place-name Society; the Environment Agency; the Forestry Commission; the Friends of Real Lancashire; the International Slavery Museum; Lancashire County Council; Lancashire County Cricket Club; the Lake District National Park Authority; Lancashire and Blackpool Tourist Board; the Merseyside Maritime Museum; the Met Office; the Museum of Lancashire; the National Football Museum; the National Piers Society; the National Trust; Natural England; the Office for National Statistics; Ordnance Survey; the Ramblers Association; the Royal Society for the Protection of Birds; Visit England; Visit Lancashire; and the Wildfowl and Wetlands Trust. I am also thankful for the help of the staff of Lancashire's wonderful libraries, especially the Lancashire Record Office in Preston.

As ever I owe most to my wife, Ceri, for her endless support and love; and to our two Lancashire-born children, Beth and Sam, for helping in all sorts of ways.

BIBLIOGRAPHY

Lancashire has a wonderfully rich tradition of literature, and I am grateful to all those authors who have researched and written about so many different aspects of Lancashire over the years. This is a selection of some of the books that were most useful to me, and I recommend them all for further reading about some of the subjects covered in this book.

Maurice Baren, *How It All Began in Lancashire* (Dalesman)

David Bellamy, *Dry Stone Walling Techniques and Traditions* (Dry Stone Walling Association)

Anthony Burton, *The Rise and Fall of King Cotton* (Deutsch)

Alan Crosby, *The Lancashire Dictionary* (Smith Settle)

Hunter Davies, *Wainwright: The Biography* (Orion)

Ron Freethy, *Lankie Twang* (Countryside Books)

Ron Freethy, *Memories of the Lancashire Cotton Mills* (Countryside Books)

Malcolm Greenhalgh, *Flavours of Lancashire: The Food and Folk of the Old County* (Palatine Books)

Dean Hayes, *Wars of the Roses: A History of Lancashire v Yorkshire Cricket Matches* (Parrs Wood Press)

Jeremy Hobson, *Curious Country Customs* (David & Charles)

Peter Hough, *Supernatural Lancashire* (Robert Hale)

Douglas Hurd, *Robert Peel* (Phoenix)

David James, *Lancashire's Lost Railways* (Stenlake)

Adam MacQueen, *The King of Sunlight: How William Lever Cleaned up the World* (Corgi)

Len Markham, *The Lancashire Weather Book* (Countryside Books)

A.D. Mills, *English Place-Names* (Oxford University Press)

David Mills, *The Place Names of Lancashire* (Batsford)

John and Anne Nuttall, *Highest Mountains: The Mountains of England and Wales Volume 2: England* (Cicerone Press)

Michael Rayner, *English Battlefields* (Tempus)

Shelley Rohde, *L.S. Lowry: A Life* (Haus Publishing)

Steve Roud, *The English Year* (Penguin)

Alfred Wainwright, *A Pictorial Guide to the Lakeland Fells Volumes 1 to 7* (Frances Lincoln)

The Chambers Book of Facts (Chambers)

The CIA 2009 World Factbook (CIA)

Guinness World Records 2010 (Guinness)

Notes on Building a Cairn: A Leaflet for the Working Waller or Dyker (Dry Stone Walling Association)

INDEX